PSALM 23: A PSALM FOR THE LIVING

23 Devotional Messages to Lead You to the Blessings of Salvation, Overflow, and Eternal Life

DR. RICKY BRANHAM

"READINGS FOR YOUR PRAYER CLOSET"
DEVOTIONAL MESSAGE SERIES — BOOK 1

TRILOGY
PROFESSIONAL PUBLISHING MEETS POWERFUL PROMOTION
A wholly owned subsidiary of TBN

Psalm 23: A Psalm for the Living | 23 Devotional Messages to Lead You to the Blessings of Salvation, Overflow, and Eternal Life

Trilogy Christian Publishers
A Wholly Owned Subsidiary of Trinity Broadcasting Network
2442 Michelle Drive, Tustin, CA 92780

Copyright © 2022 by Dr. Ricky Branham
www.rickybranham.com

All scripture quotations are taken from the King James Version of the Bible. Public domain.

No part of this book may be reproduced, stored in a retrieval system, or transmitted by any means without written permission from the author. All rights reserved. Printed in the USA. Rights Department, 2442 Michelle Drive, Tustin, CA 92780.

Trilogy Christian Publishing/TBN and colophon are trademarks of Trinity Broadcasting Network.

Photography by: Christie Stevens Photography & Holiday Photography

For information about special discounts for bulk purchases, please contact Trilogy Christian Publishing.

Trilogy Disclaimer: The views and content expressed in this book are those of the author and may not necessarily reflect the views and doctrine of Trilogy Christian Publishing or the Trinity Broadcasting Network.

Manufactured in the United States of America
10 9 8 7 6 5 4 3 2 1
Library of Congress Cataloging-in-Publication Data is available.

ISBN: 978-1-68556-891-7
E-ISBN: 978-1-68556-892-4

DEDICATION

To my beautiful, smart, and adoring wife, Victoria. Your support is immeasurable, and you are a true example of a Proverbs 31 wife and mother.

To our kids, Ricky, Riley, and Vera, whom I know God has amazing things planned for. The joy you have brought to our home is fulfilling. Always remember to let God be your Shepherd, and you will experience His blessings of salvation, overflow, and eternal life.

To my grandparents in Heaven, Robert and Lena Branham, who taught me the ways and things of God from a young age.

ACKNOWLEDGMENTS

Thanks to my mother, father, step-father, and step-mother, which have stood behind my calling from the beginning.

Thanks to my brother, Joshua Branham, for his listening ear, editing and graphic designing, and for supporting my ministry in every way.

Thanks to Robert Holthouse of Robert Holthouse Productions, who uses his video production talents to help me spread the Word of God all over the world.

Thanks to Dr. Tony V. Lewis and Christian Bible Institute & Seminary for their encouragement, education, and continued support.

CONTENT

Dedication v
Acknowledgments vii

Introduction 11
How to Read the Devotional Messages 15
How the Lord Leads 31
Psalm 23 33

Blessing #1: Salvation 35
Devotional 1: The LORD Is My Shepherd 37

Blessing #2: Overflow 43
Devotional 2: I Shall Not Want 45
Devotional 3: He Maketh Me to Lie Down
               in Green Pastures. 53
Devotional 4: He Leadeth Me Beside the Still Waters . . 59
Devotional 5: He Restoreth My Soul 65
Devotional 6: He Leadeth Me in the Paths of
               Righteousness 71
Devotional 7: For His Name's Sake 79
Devotional 8: Yea, Though I Walk through the
               Valley of the Shadow of Death 85
Devotional 9: I Will Fear No Evil 91
Devotional 10: For Thou Art with Me 97
Devotional 11: Thy Rod and Thy Staff 103
Devotional 12: They Comfort Me 111

Devotional 13: Thou Preparest 117
Devotional 14: A Table Before Me. 123
Devotional 15: In the Presence of Mine Enemies 129
Devotional 16: Thou Anointest My Head with Oil . . . 137
Devotional 17: My Cup Runneth Over 145
Devotional 18: Surely 155
Devotional 19: Goodness and Mercy 161
Devotional 20: Shall Follow Me 167
Devotional 21: All the Days of My Life 173

Blessing #3: Eternal Life. 179
Devotional 22: And I Will Dwell in the House of the
                LORD 181
Devotional 23: For Ever 189

How the Lord Became My Shepherd 195
Bibliography. 207

Coming Soon 209
Contacts/Television/Social Media. 211

INTRODUCTION

Do you need a miracle spiritually, physically, mentally, emotionally, relationally, or financially? God has your miracle and wants to deliver it to you quickly. Your answer can be found in the most popular psalm, which is Psalm 23. This is a psalm for the living. It is a mini-Bible because in six short verses, you will be led to receive God's blessings of salvation, overflow, and eternal life.

I break down Psalm 23 into twenty-three devotional messages. Each devotional message contains a central biblical theme, many Bible scriptures, and a message from God for you. You are reading a small sermon in many regards. The messages can be read anywhere and anytime to help you grow in the Lord. They can also be used to help prepare sermons, Sunday school lessons, and for general Bible discussions. However, you will find the most value in them when they are read in your prayer closet. God will use them to speak to you in a powerful way during this quiet time with Him, and it will change your life forever. Be ready to receive the blessings of salvation, overflow, and eternal life.

Why Psalm 23?

I have always sought to know God in a deeper way. In March of 2020, when the pandemic really started to hit the world hard, I started seeking God like never before in my prayer closet, also known as my bedroom. As a result, I started to have new revelations from God's Word and many dreams from God. One night I dreamt that I was at a church service, and the minister gave the message, "We are all God's sheep." In the dream as the minister gave the message, you could feel God's love and peace move throughout the congregation. This dream was part of the inspiration for this book.

As a minister, I know the power and impact of Psalm 23, which is arguably the most famous chapter in the Bible in regards to God our Shepherd. I have read this chapter countless times. It is the most requested psalm to be read at funerals because it is so widely known and beloved. Society views this psalm more as a message for those who have gone on to be with the Lord. As I later meditated and prayed about the dream He gave me, God strongly revealed to me the message of this psalm is really for the living. It is a psalm for the living. Psalm 23 has everything a person will need in life and is full of promises that can be claimed right now. It is a mini-Bible because in only six verses it contains the desires of God for mankind through His blessings of salvation, overflow, and eternal life. This revelation from God was part of the inspiration for this book.

The final idea for this book came together when I was looking for devotionals for my family members for Christmas. I ordered numerous Christian devotionals with the idea that I would pick the best one and then buy multiple copies to give out. I was saddened as I combed through these Christian devotionals finding they lacked depth and clear messages. One of the "Christian" devotionals did not even quote a Bible scripture. I felt led by God to write a devotional message book based on the revealed Word of Psalm 23. I want each devotional message to enlighten you with a deeper meaning of this beloved psalm, be biblically based, and to be used when possible in your quiet time with God. This is the first book in my series "Readings for Your Prayer Closet" because each devotional message will especially bless your alone time with God. I will explain more in the next section.

HOW TO READ THE DEVOTIONAL MESSAGES

People are starting to become hungry for the presence of God because they need the power of God in their lives. They need Him to save, heal, bless, and perform miracles, which can all happen in His mighty presence. God's presence is everywhere (Psalm 139:7–12) but you may not recognize it or realize it. When I start talking about God's presence arriving, the pathway into God's presence, finding God's presence, being taken into God's presence, and God showing up, I am saying that God makes you aware of His presence. In other words, God reveals Himself to you to let you know He is there.

God will show up, and when He does, He can let you know He is there in a variety of ways. You may know His presence by feeling Him. He may press something on your heart by giving you a godly thought, idea, or answer to a problem or situation. He may make the Word of God come alive to you. You may hear an audible voice, have a vision, or fall asleep and have a godly dream. He may appear by healing your body, giving you peace, or giving you rest. He may answer one or several of your prayers. He may send someone to speak a word from God to you. He may open or close a door of opportunity. In whatever way God decides to tell you He is there, you will know He is with you.

God promised in Acts 2:17 that He would pour out His Spirit upon all flesh in the last days. We are in the last days, so now is the time for you to experience the power of the presence of God. So, where do you find God's presence? This could be a deep theological discussion, but it does not need to be because finding God's presence is simple. First, let me begin by going over a few basic biblical principles about the presence of God.

Three Basic Principles about the Presence of God

1. God sees everything the sinner and the saint do. In other words, God's presence is everywhere.

   The eyes of the LORD are in every place, beholding the evil and the good.
   —Proverbs 15:3

2. The Spirit of God lives in the believer. In other words, God's presence is in the Christian.

   But ye are not in the flesh, but in the Spirit, if so be that the Spirit of God dwell in you. Now if any man have not the Spirit of Christ, he is none of His.
   —Romans 8:9

3. God promises to never leave nor forsake the one who remains in Christ. In other words, God's presence will never be taken from one of His children.

   […] For He hath said, "I will never leave thee, nor forsake thee."
   —Hebrews 13:5

How I Discovered A Pathway into the Presence of God

I have felt, seen, and known a strong presence of God on a variety of occasions and various situations. I have seen the power and might of God move in mighty ways inside the church. He has spoken to my heart on many occasions inside the church. I felt the call of God to become a preacher when I was fifteen at a church service. I have seen God move when it has just been my wife and I praying. I have also experienced the power of God by myself. He has told me many things when it has been just Him and I. What is the best way to experience God's presence and hear His voice regularly? God taught me through His leading and His Word how to practice the palpable presence of God consistently, as I will show you soon.

As I alluded to earlier in my introduction chapter, I have always sought God. However, I started seeking God during the beginning of the pandemic in March of 2020 like never before by going regularly into my prayer closet. I started seeking God like this because of the immense desire that I had to want to know Him in a deeper way. God's Holy Spirit was drawing me to spend time alone with Him. I came across these Bible verses in Matthew that I have read numerous times. However, the Spirit of God used these scriptures to confirm the drawing I felt.

> *And when thou prayest, thou shalt not be as the hypocrites are: for they love to pray standing in the synagogues and in the corners of the streets, that they may be seen of men. Verily I say unto you, They have their reward. But thou, when thou prayest, enter into thy*

closet, and when thou hast shut thy door, pray to thy Father which is in secret; and thy Father which seeth in secret shall reward thee openly.

—Matthew 6:5–6

It was during these alone times I discovered a pathway into God's presence. Notice I said "a" pathway, not the only pathway. God can take you into His presence in many ways. However, every road you take into His presence must begin with Jesus Christ. There are no exceptions to that rule. In other words, everything starts with Jesus. Here is a powerful pathway that I have used many times, and it has always worked for me. I know it will work for you.

A Pathway into the Presence of God

Each step is filled with glorious spiritual experiences. Keep progressing through the steps until God reveals His presence to you, and He will. Once you experience God's presence, let Him lead you as to whether or not you continue with the remaining steps. You may experience Him in one, two, or several of the steps. He may cause you to go back and do one or several of the steps again. Or His presence may just leave you speechless and in awe of Him.

1. JESUS CHRIST MUST BE YOUR LORD AND PERSONAL SAVIOR

Do you need and want to repent (ask God for forgiveness and turn from sin), confess (with your mouth out loud), and accept Jesus Christ as your Lord (master, owner, or ruler) and personal

Savior (one that saves believers from their sins and gives them a home in Heaven)? Maybe you are already a Christian but do you want to rededicate your life to Him? If you are not a Christian or already are a Christian but you want to rededicate your life to Him, this is what you need to know and do:

a. We have all sinned.

> *For all have sinned, and come short of the glory of God.*
> —Romans 3:23

b. God loves you.

> *For God so loved the world, that He gave His only begotten Son, that whosoever believeth in Him should not perish, but have everlasting life.*
> —John 3:16

c. God wants everyone to go to Heaven.

> *The Lord is not slack concerning His promise, as some men count slackness; but is longsuffering to us-ward, not willing that any should perish, but that all should come to repentance.*
> —2 Peter 3:9

d. Jesus Christ is the only way to Heaven.

> *Jesus saith unto him, "I am the way, the truth, and the life: no man cometh unto the Father, but by Me."*
> —John 14:6

e. You must repent, confess, and accept Jesus Christ as your Lord and personal Savior.

From that time Jesus began to preach and to say, Repent: for the kingdom of Heaven is at hand.
—Matthew 4:17

That if thou shalt confess with thy mouth the Lord Jesus, and shalt believe in thine heart that God hath raised Him from the dead, thou shalt be saved.
—Romans 10:9

For whosoever shall call upon the name of the Lord shall be saved.
—Romans 10:13

f. Today is the day of salvation.

For He saith, "I have heard thee in a time accepted, and in the day of salvation have I succoured thee: behold, now is the accepted time; behold, now is the day of salvation."
—2 Corinthians 6:2

g. You can repent, confess, and accept Jesus Christ as your Lord and personal Savior by praying out loud and believing this prayer (The Prayer of Salvation) anywhere, anytime, and with anyone around:

"Dear Heavenly Father, I confess, and I believe that Jesus Christ died on the cross for my sins, and on the third day, You raised Him from the dead. I confess, and I accept Jesus Christ as my Lord and personal

Savior. I invite Jesus into my heart and into my life. I ask You, God, to forgive me of all my sins, and I forgive everyone. I ask You to save me, to help me, to change me, and to give me a home in Heaven. I ask all of this in Jesus' name. Amen."

Congratulations! The Lord is your personal Savior. Live for Him by daily praying to God in the name of Jesus, by attending a Bible-believing church, and by reading your Bible.

Now you are a born-again Christian and living for God. You do not need to keep repeating The Prayer of Salvation. However, make no mistake about it; if you want to experience the greatness of His presence and His blessings, you have to be living for Him and make sure there is nothing between you and Him. If you are a Christian but think that there is something hindering your relationship with God, then confess your sins by asking God to forgive you in the name of Jesus (1 John 1:9). This will clear the channel to ensure that you can hear from God clearly. You can go to your prayer closet in peace, knowing that you are saved, and you are His child.

2. BE ALONE WITH GOD IN YOUR PRAYER CLOSET

To regularly experience the presence of God that I am talking about, you will need to go to your prayer closet regularly alone. Whether you call it a prayer closet, prayer room, secret room, or secret chamber, it does not matter. This may be your bedroom, bathroom, or chapel, and it does not matter where it is. It just matters that you are alone with God and are free from all distractions. I know life is busy, but you must schedule time to be alone with Him. I just quoted this verse earlier, but it is already worth repeating:

> *But thou, when thou prayest, enter into thy closet, and when thou hast shut thy door, pray to thy Father which is in secret; and thy Father which seeth in secret shall reward thee openly.*
>
> —Matthew 6:6

I look forward to being alone with God. It is not a task, it is not difficult, and it is not burdensome. Rather, it is restful, easy, and a relief. I find myself wanting to spend more and more time with God alone. I try to do this regularly and sometimes multiple times a day because it is such a wonderful time of fellowship.

3. PRAY

Why does God tell you to be alone? So you can pray to Him in the name of Jesus (John 14:13–14). Therefore, start your alone time with God by talking and praying to Him as Jesus did.

> *And when He had sent the multitudes away, He went up into a mountain apart to pray: and when the evening was come, He was there alone.*
>
> —Matthew 14:23

Ask God for whatsoever it is you desire because God does not place limitations on what you ask for; just believe.

> *Ask, and it shall be given you; seek and ye shall find; knock, and it shall be opened unto you.*
>
> —Matthew 7:7

> *Therefore I say unto you, "What things soever ye desire, when ye pray, believe that ye receive them, and ye shall have them."*
> —Mark 11:24

Your prayers might change based on what is going on in your life. Sometimes I will pray for my family, friends, churches, and ministry partners. Sometimes I will ask God for what I need, what I want, and what I desire because God cares about everything.

> *Casting all your care upon Him; for He careth for you.*
> —1 Peter 5:7

Sometimes I will ask God to show me His ways and teach me His paths.

> *Shew me Thy ways, O LORD; teach me Thy paths.*
> —Psalm 25:4

4. THANKSGIVING/PRAISE/WORSHIP

Move from praying to giving God thanks. Giving God thanks means expressing gratitude to Him for all that He has done and all that He will do.

> *Be careful for nothing; but in every thing by prayer and supplication with thanksgiving let your requests be made known unto God.*
> —Philippians 4:6

Daniel gave God thanks after he prayed.

> *Now when Daniel knew that the writing was signed, he went into his house; and his windows being open in his chamber toward Jerusalem, he kneeled upon his knees three times a day, and prayed, and gave thanks before his God, as he did aforetime.*
>
> —Daniel 6:10

After giving thanks, move into praising God, which means to bless, glorify, or magnify Him because of His mighty acts and His excellent greatness (Psalm 150:2).

> *Enter into His gates with thanksgiving, and into His courts with praise: be thankful unto Him, and bless His name.*
>
> —Psalm 100:4

Notice that when you enter the gates, you give thanks. The deeper you go, the courts, then you give praise. After giving God praise, the deeper you go leads to worshipping God, which means to bow down in reverence because of His holiness and this should be done in the fear of the LORD (Psalm 96:9).

> *God is a Spirit: and they that worship Him must worship Him in spirit and in truth.*
>
> —John 4:24

Even though I will oftentimes start with giving God thanks, then move to praise, then to worship, sometimes I will start with praise or worship. I may be worshiping God, then I go back to giving thanks, then I move to praise. As the Spirit of God stirs during this time, you may naturally flow from one to another and back to one, then back to another without even realizing it.

5. READ YOUR BIBLE AND/OR DEVOTIONAL MESSAGE, THEN MEDITATE

Reading Bible scriptures must be incorporated into your alone time. The best way to do this is by directly reading Bible scriptures, which is why my books contain numerous Bible verses. I call my devotional message series "Readings for Your Prayer Closet." My devotional messages have a central biblical theme, many Bible scriptures, and a message from God. You are reading a small sermon in many regards. I pray God uses my books to speak His Word to you.

As you are reading, the Spirit of God will make something stand out. A scripture(s) and/or theme will catch your attention and really speak to you, which is what you meditate upon. Meditation means to think deeply about or to focus on. Meditation is a biblical principle that God requires.

> *This book of the law shall not depart out of thy mouth; but thou shalt meditate therein day and night, that thou mayest observe to do according to all that is written therein: for then thou shalt make thy way prosperous, and then thou shalt have good success.*
> —Joshua 1:8

How much you read will depend on what is on your heart and mind. Always try to meditate by focusing on and repeating the part(s) that speaks to you. You may do this by reciting a verse and/or by breaking down a verse, section, or theme into smaller parts and thinking about it. Do this with the part that God uses to speak to your heart.

The reason my devotional message series is called "Readings for Your Prayer Closet" is because they are designed to be read when you are alone with God in your prayer closet and free from distractions. The best time to read them is during this quiet time before you start waiting on God (next section). However, they can be read anywhere and anytime. Many will use the insights in them while at work, during Sunday school, or for sermons.

6. WAITING ON GOD

You are a Christian, you are alone with God and free from distractions in your prayer closet, you have prayed, gave God thanks, praise, and worship, and read and meditated upon the Scriptures. You may have already experienced God's presence in one of these steps, glory be to God. However, if you have not yet experienced His presence, you are now to wait on Him. Waiting on God is something that is not taught and preached on enough. God is not rushed. He will speak and move when He is ready, so you must be ready. Jesus taught His disciples the principle of waiting to experience God's presence and power.

> *And, behold, I send the promise of my Father upon you: but tarry ye in the city of Jerusalem, until ye be endued with power from on high.*
>
> —Luke 24:49

You may be asking, "What should I do while I wait on God during these alone times?" First, become silent before God by no longer speaking because it is time to hear from God when He moves.

> *Be silent, O all flesh, before the LORD: for He is raised up out of His holy habitation.*
>
> —Zechariah 2:13

Second, become "still." According to the Hebrew word *raphah* (7503), stillness means to be still, relax, or sink. I become still by slowing my breathing and resting my body and mind.

> *Be still, and know that I am God [...].*
> —Psalm 46:10

Lastly, wait patiently for Him to move. Sometimes He moves almost immediately. Other times it may be ten minutes, thirty minutes, or an hour. God is not rushed. Obviously, there are times when you cannot wait a long time because of obligations you may have. However, do your best to wait on Him as long as you can.

> *Rest in the LORD, and wait patiently for Him [...].*
> —Psalm 37:7

The Holy Spirit Will Reveal Himself

God the Holy Spirit will show up, and when He does, He can let you know He is there in a variety of ways. You may know His presence by feeling Him. He may press something on your heart by giving you a godly thought, idea, or answer to a problem or situation. He may make the Word of God come alive to you. You may hear an audible voice, have a vision, or fall asleep and have a godly dream. He may appear by healing your body, giving you peace, or giving you rest. He may answer one or several of your prayers. He may send someone to speak a word from God to you. He may open or close a door of opportunity. In whatever way the Holy Spirit decides to tell you He is there, you will know He is with you.

My sheep hear my voice, and I know them, and they follow me.

—John 10:27

Remember, you can experience God's presence in one, two, or several of the steps I mentioned. Furthermore, His presence may cause you to go back and do one or several of the steps again. Or His presence may just leave you speechless and in awe of Him.

Summary

God sees everything that goes on in the world. His presence lives in His children. He will not turn His back on them. He desires for you to know Him in a deeper way, which causes you to experience the majesty of His presence in a meaningful way. Anywhere, anytime, and with anyone around, you can experience God. However, I have found the best way to regularly experience God's presence is by regularly following the process I have shared with you. Your process may vary when it comes to what you do in order to experience God's presence. However, knowing Jesus Christ as your Lord and personal Savior is a must.

One of the main pathways that I have found to become familiar with His Divine Spirit works. First, make sure you are right with God. If you are a sinner, pray The Prayer of Salvation. If you are a Christian but have unconfessed sins, ask God to forgive you of all your sins. Then go to a room where you are alone, where it is quiet and free from distractions. Start to pray and talk with God. Next, give Him thanks, praise, and worship. Then, read and meditate upon God's Word. Finally, wait on

God by becoming silent, still, and patient until the Holy Spirit reveals Himself. Remember, it can vary as to the order of when you pray, when you give God thanks/praise/worship, when you read and meditate upon the Bible, and when you wait on Him. If the Spirit of God has not yet spoken or moved in your process, let the Spirit of God lead you. The important thing is that you follow His leading and allow Him to influence your steps into His presence.

The Holy Spirit arrives with mighty blessings. He may bring with Him healings, miracles, and answers. He is God, and that is what He does. Whenever the presence of God arrives, you are never the same. It is impossible to experience God and not be changed. His presence may cause you to flow in and out of the previous steps or leave you in amazement. Remember, you can read these devotional messages anywhere and anytime. Read them as part of your pathway into the presence of God. Watch the power of God manifest in your life.

HOW THE LORD LEADS

You will see all throughout my book that the Lord leads. Psalm 23 teaches you about the blessings that the Lord leads you to, which I have categorized as Salvation, Overflow, and Eternal Life. The blessings that you obtain from Psalm 23 are the focus of my book.

I want to give you some simple examples of how the Lord may lead you. Oftentimes, the Lord leads by making you aware of His presence. His presence helps you to know His will, and this leads you to one or more of His promises. God can lead you to His blessings by having you feel His presence; pressing something on your heart by giving you a godly thought, idea, or answer to a problem or situation; making the Word of God come alive; hearing an audible voice; having a vision; having a godly dream; healing your body; giving peace; giving rest; answering one or several prayers; sending someone to speak a word from God to you and opening or closing a door of opportunity. The Lord will lead you the way He wants to because He knows what is best. His leading will always take you to His glorious blessings.

Be on the lookout for God to reveal His presence to you. Get ready to be led and get ready to receive all that God has planned for you.

PSALM 23

The LORD is my shepherd; I shall not want.

He maketh me to lie down in green pastures: He leadeth me beside the still waters.

He restoreth my soul: He leadeth me in the paths of righteousness for His name's sake.

Yea, though I walk through the valley of the shadow of death, I will fear no evil: for Thou art with me; Thy rod and Thy staff they comfort me.

Thou preparest a table before me in the presence of mine enemies: Thou anointest my head with oil; my cup runneth over.

Surely goodness and mercy shall follow me all the days of my life: and I will dwell in the house of the LORD for ever.

BLESSING #1

Salvation

Having a personal relationship with Jesus Christ because He has forgiven you of your sins, and He is your Lord and personal Savior. Salvation begins on Earth.

DEVOTIONAL 1

The LORD Is My Shepherd

The LORD is my shepherd; *I shall not want.*

—Psalm 23:1

Do you desire for you and your family to have a better life in every way? I know you do because God has led you to this book for a reason. The answer to your desire starts with Jesus Christ becoming your Shepherd. I accepted Jesus as my Shepherd when I was fifteen, and that is one decision I have never regretted. I have never met anyone yet who has regretted that decision. However, I have met a lot of people who wished they would have started serving God earlier. Jesus is the key that unlocks the blessings of God in your life. He starts by bringing you to salvation through His Spirit, which gives your spirit the rest it has been looking for. He then blesses you with overflow on earth, which are abundant blessings from Him. His blessings include every area of your life: spiritually, physically, mentally, emotionally, relationally, and financially. He then will lead you to eternal life. God's plan is bigger and better than you could ever imagine. I am excited to show you these truths throughout these upcoming devotional messages. Now it is time to learn that the Shepherd leads you, the sheep, to spiritual rest through salvation. This spiritual rest is only possible by repenting, confessing, and accepting Jesus Christ as your Lord and personal Savior. This is the starting point to receiving all that God has for you.

King David, who I also at times call the Psalmist, wrote this mini-Bible of a psalm under the divine inspiration of God. The psalm opens up by revealing that God has to be the starting point to have a great life. This is why David opens with "The LORD." The King James Bible sometimes capitalizes all the letters of the word "LORD" so I will capitalize the same way when quoting scriptures that do. The Hebrew word for "LORD" in this verse is *YHWH* (3068), which is the name of God meaning Lord, Jehovah, Yahweh, the Self-Existent, or the Eternal. The Hebrew name of God notes a personal relationship with mankind through salvation. In other words, God wants a personal relationship with His creation. That is why the Lord wants to be your Shepherd. He is not a God that is far off in a distant land that cannot be reached or experienced. He is a close God, a personal God. The God who created everything and everyone desires to be near His creation. *Wow!* Let that sink in for a moment.

David says that the Lord "is," which when you are reading you would not even pause for this little word. However, the word "is" in this case is a powerful word. It serves as a reminder of His present tense. It is not a past tense or a future tense but a right now tense. The Lord is here and now. Many Christians pray for something believing that eventually, down the road, or someday, God will answer or come through. Yes, sometimes you do have to wait for the proper season, but many times God wants to move right now. He wants you to have faith right now because He is a now God.

Notice the personal pronoun "my," which indicates David's acceptance of the Lord's desire to be close to His creation. I chose the word "acceptance" carefully because it is the Spirit of God that draws, but it is the individual who must accept the Spirit's drawing. David had a connection with God. David had a special relationship with Him because he did not say that He was a shepherd or one shepherd or some shepherd. He says He is "my" Shepherd. The words chosen by the Psalmist reveal the psalm as a conditional chapter. In other words, do not expect to receive anything if you do not have a personal relationship with God through Jesus Christ because the rest of the passage will not apply to you. You have to meet the condition to receive the blessing.

Once you meet the condition of salvation that is only through Jesus Christ, you will be able to say "the LORD is my Shepherd." The Hebrew word for "Shepherd" is *ra'ah* (7462), which means to shepherd, tend to, feed, or associate with. God is clear that He wants to lead you in every way. He wants to take care of you. He wants to have fellowship with you. Think about it, the God who created everything wants to be directly involved with you. He wants to lead you into His overflow of blessings on earth and in eternal life. First, you have to start by making Him your Shepherd because only He knows the way to blessings or overflow on earth and the way to eternal life. The way to make Him your Shepherd is to repent, confess, and accept Jesus Christ as your Lord and personal Savior.

The Lord Your Shepherd

Do you need and want to repent (ask God for forgiveness and turn from sin), confess (with your mouth out loud), and accept

Jesus Christ as your Lord (master, owner, or ruler) and personal Savior (one that saves believers from their sins and gives them a home in Heaven)? Maybe you are already a Christian but do you want to rededicate your life to Him? If you are not a Christian or already are a Christian but you want to rededicate your life to Him, this is what you need to know and do:

a. We have all sinned.

> *For all have sinned, and come short of the glory of God.*
>
> —Romans 3:23

b. God loves you.

> *For God so loved the world, that He gave His only begotten Son, that whosoever believeth in Him should not perish, but have everlasting life.*
>
> —John 3:16

c. God wants everyone to go to Heaven.

> *The Lord is not slack concerning His promise, as some men count slackness; but is longsuffering to us-ward, not willing that any should perish, but that all should come to repentance.*
>
> —2 Peter 3:9

d. Jesus Christ is the only way to Heaven.

> *Jesus saith unto him, "I am the way, the truth, and the life: no man cometh unto the Father, but by Me."*
>
> —John 14:6

e. You must repent, confess, and accept Jesus Christ as your Lord and personal Savior.

From that time Jesus began to preach and to say, "Repent: for the kingdom of Heaven is at hand."
—Matthew 4:17

That if thou shalt confess with thy mouth the Lord Jesus, and shalt believe in thine heart that God hath raised Him from the dead, thou shalt be saved.
—Romans 10:9

For whosoever shall call upon the name of the Lord shall be saved.
—Romans 10:13

f. Today is the day of salvation.

For He saith, "I have heard thee in a time accepted, and in the day of salvation have I succoured thee: behold, now is the accepted time; behold, now is the day of salvation."
—2 Corinthians 6:2

g. You can repent, confess, and accept Jesus Christ as your Lord and personal Savior by praying out loud and believing this prayer (The Prayer of Salvation) anywhere, anytime, and with anyone around:

"Dear Heavenly Father, I confess and I believe that Jesus Christ died on the cross for my sins, and on the third day, You raised Him from the dead. I confess, and I accept Jesus Christ as my Lord and personal

Savior. I invite Jesus into my heart and into my life. I ask You, God, to forgive me of all my sins, and I forgive everyone. I ask You to save me, to help me, to change me, and to give me a home in Heaven. I ask all of this in Jesus' name. Amen."

Congratulations! The Lord is your personal Savior. Live for Him by daily praying to God in the name of Jesus, by attending a Bible-believing church, and by reading your Bible.

Now that you are a born-again Christian and living for Him, He is your Shepherd. You do not need to keep repeating The Prayer of Salvation. However, make no mistake about it; if you want to experience the greatness of His presence and His blessings, you have to be living for Him and make sure there is nothing between you and Him. If you are a Christian but think that there is something hindering your relationship with God, then confess your sins by asking God to forgive you in the name of Jesus (1 John 1:9). This will clear the channel to ensure that you can hear from God clearly.

You now have the spiritual rest that the Shepherd promised. God will lead you to His blessings of overflow on this earth and His blessings of eternal life in Heaven. What a blessing of God! Later in this book, I will share with you "How the Lord Became My Shepherd."

Declaration of Faith

God, I thank You for taking me into Your fold. From this moment on, I know I will experience all the great things You have for me as You lead me forever.

BLESSING #2
Overflow

God's blessings of abundance in your life while on earth.

DEVOTIONAL 2

I Shall Not Want

The LORD is my shepherd; **I shall not want.**
—Psalm 23:1

You probably have not heard or read a lot of sermons on the subject of not wanting, although it is clearly an overflowing blessing of God. To "not want" means that you have everything you want. God wants to give you everything you want as long as it aligns with His will and Word. In my humble opinion, you have not heard or read a lot on the subject of not wanting because it goes against the way society wants to portray Christians. Society lies to you by saying Christianity is: hard, you have to struggle and be poor, do not tell what God has done or else you are prideful, and you should only ask for what you need; otherwise, you are being greedy. Unfortunately, this mentality is very strong in many Christian circles also.

If you do believe that God desires for you to have everything you want, then you are labeled a "prosperity" preacher-believer, which is supposed to have a negative connotation. The question I ask you is why is it wrong to believe in the principle of not wanting. David understood it is not wrong to believe and ask God for your heart's desires as long as it lines up with God's will and Word. David states the importance of not wanting by making it the first thing he says after one receives spiritual rest through salvation. The Shepherd has given you, the sheep, spiritual rest through salvation. Now it is time to learn that God leads you to no longer want, as long as your wants align with His will and His Word.

The devil has a plan to keep Christians depressed, suppressed, oppressed, and repressed. He wants them to be weak, be divided, and have confusion. He is trying to get you to think that God is harsh, cruel, and stingy. He wants you to believe that God does not want you to be blessed and prosper. If the devil can succeed in getting you to believe any of these lies, then you will not pray as much and will be less likely to put your faith, hope, and trust in God. Also, you will not be encouraged to tell others about Jesus if you view the Christian life as difficult and burdensome. The good news is that God is the exact opposite.

The first statement David made in the psalm concerns salvation, which is spiritual rest. Obviously, the number one goal in this life is to get to Heaven, which is why it is worth repeating. This is what your focus should be and where your treasure should be.

> *For where your treasure is, there will your heart be also.*
>
> —Matthew 6:21

It is clear you are to seek the kingdom of God first, which means the sovereignty of God over everything. In simpler terms, seek God and His will first.

> *But seek ye first the kingdom of God, and His righteousness; and all these things shall be added unto you.*
>
> —Matthew 6:33

If you seek God the way He desires, He will bless you. David is showing that after salvation, God can make it where you do not want.

The Hebrew word to "not want" is *chaser* (2637), which means to want or lack. The Bible is clear, let God be your Shepherd, and you will not lack anything. God wants to give you whatever you need, want, and desire to accomplish what He has called you to. God can make it where you no longer want by doing a couple of things. First, He can give you contentment and peace so that you no longer desire to have things that are outside the will of God. He can make you satisfied with your house, your job, and everything else in life that He has blessed you with. God can make you content, and that is a tremendous blessing from Him.

> *But godliness with contentment is great gain.*
> —1 Timothy 6:6

The second way that God can make it where you no longer want is by answering your prayers. If you are truly following Christ to the best of your ability, seeking after Him, growing in Him, and having your focus on Him, you may still have wants because God placed them there. If you have godly wants, also known as godly desires, it is because God wants to bless you in a greater way. Let me say it another way because it is important to understand this: God wants to answer your wants and desires because you are putting Him first. Therefore, His desires and your desires match, so you should pray asking and believing. He will answer your prayers for His glory.

God's original plan for man was that He put Adam and Eve in a luscious garden where they could have anything they desired, except from one tree. God has not changed. There are countless scriptures that show you it is the will of God to bless you greatly. One of my favorites is Psalm 23:1, but I will share with you several of my other favorites.

> *Ask, and it shall be given you; seek, and ye shall find; knock, and it shall be opened unto you.*
>
> —Matthew 7:7

> *But Jesus beheld them, and said unto them, "With men this is impossible; but with God all things are possible."*
>
> —Matthew 19:26

> *For verily I say unto you, That whosoever shall say unto this mountain, Be thou removed, and be thou cast into the sea; and shall not doubt in his heart, but shall believe that those things which he saith shall come to pass, he shall have whatsoever he saith. Therefore, I say unto you, What things soever ye desire, when ye pray, believe that ye receive them, and ye shall have them.*
>
> —Mark 11:23–24

> *The thief cometh not, but for to steal, and to kill, and to destroy: I am come that they might have life, and that they might have it more abundantly.*
>
> —John 10:10

> *Beloved, I wish above all things that thou mayest prosper and be in health, even as thy soul prospereth.*
>
> —3 John 1:2

God showed me His desire to bless me materially. I have been a serious Christian since I was fifteen years old and have never turned my back on Him. Although I have not been perfect, I have been extremely serious about serving God to the best of my ability. As I started to grow in the Lord, God used a newer-used car to show me His desire to bless me materially. My first three cars were, let's just say, only good enough to get me from point A to point B. However, I always felt blessed to have a car despite the numerous breakdowns, continual leaking of oil, and no air conditioning. I was content. However, one day I drove by a car lot and saw a used car that really caught my attention. I went home and prayed about it. Did I need it? No, I had a car; even though it was literally missing the front bumper, it was still a car though that did the job. I prayed and prayed and had such a desire to have this newer car. I realized that God wanted me to have it. I went to the dealership, got a great price, and drove home in a new to me 2007 Blue Cadillac Catera. It had an air conditioner and did not leak any fluids—what a blessing. I drove it to my mentor's church where he pastored, and all at once, I felt guilty. I explained to him that I had prayed and had this desire, and I really believed it to be from God. He said to me something that I did not expect. He told me that to have something nice is not a sin, but it is the will of God that His children be blessed. I breathed a sigh of relief that I had heard from God. I was not being greedy; God just loved me.

As I continued to grow more in the Lord, I found that God wanted to bless me more than I realized. God showed me that I was not praying and believing big enough. He started laying bigger things on my heart to pray and believe for. I did, and He answered. Not so that I could brag or show off, but because He loved me. God has continued to give me my wants and desires because they are in line with His will and Word. The same thing happened in my spiritual walk.

God showed me His desire to bless me spiritually. I was content being faithful to God, spreading His Word in smaller churches. However, I believed for too little when God wanted to use me to accomplish bigger things for His kingdom. Once I accepted that God had bigger plans, the floodgates of Christian television, radio, media, books, and other opportunities opened. I started to have a tremendous want and desire to win one million people to Jesus in my lifetime. In my first year on television, more people came to know Jesus Christ as their Lord and personal Savior than in my previous twenty-one years of ministering combined. I was not being greedy; God was simply wanting to use me in a mighty way for His glory because He loved me.

Are you putting the Shepherd first in every area of your life, yet you have a desire for something better or more? God has probably put that desire in you and is just waiting for you to ask and believe Him for it. Yes, you could live like Mother Teresa and not own anything. Technically, you do not need a car, you only need a little shack, and you only need a few items of clothing. However, God, as your Father and Shepherd, wants to give you more because He loves you in the same way you want to take care of your kids. Stop feeling guilty for asking and believing for things from God. Stop questioning if it is God's will when He has clearly shown you it is His will. Everyone around you may say, "Watch out because you are doing something wrong" or "You're becoming greedy." However, God says, "If I put a want in you that is in alignment with My will and Word, it is meant for you to have." Never apologize for God's blessings but instead remember three scriptures, and you will stay on the right path:

> *Beware that thou forget not the LORD thy God [...].*
> —Deuteronomy 8:11

> *Every good gift and every perfect gift is from above, and cometh down from the Father of lights, with whom is no variableness, neither shadow of turning.*
> —James 1:17

> *Even every one that is called by my name: for I have created Him for my glory, I have formed him; yea, I have made him.*
> —Isaiah 43:7

David was saved and states that he would not want. You are saved, and you will not want. This is only the beginning of God's overflow to you on earth. What a blessing of God!

Pray

> *"Dear Heavenly Father, please help me to seek You first always in everything I do. My first want is to please You. I know You have great things in store for me, so please help me to receive those things in the seasons and ways You would have me to. May all this be done for Your glory alone. I ask all of this in Jesus' name. Amen."*

Declaration of Faith

God, I thank You for Your abundant blessings that You want me to have and that are coming my way quickly.

DEVOTIONAL 3

He Maketh Me to Lie Down in Green Pastures

He maketh me to lie down in green pastures: *He leadeth me beside the still waters.*

—Psalm 23:2

The moment I read verse two, it seems as if I can picture it. A beautiful open area full of green grass with the sun shining comes to mind. What a stunning promise of God for His children that causes me to want this experience. There is nothing difficult or sad about this pasture. It is a pasture of rest and blessings. It is a place that I want God to lead me to. The Shepherd has given you, the sheep, spiritual rest through salvation, and you no longer want. Now it is time to learn that God leads you to a place of physical rest.

It starts with "He." You cannot find this place of rest on your own because you do not know where it is. You cannot find Heaven on your own. The Shepherd has to lead you. Society has spent billions of dollars on self-help books, counseling, and medications looking for that place of peace and rest, but it cannot be found outside of God. To be clear, God can use

Christian counselors and doctors and medication to help with problems, but it still takes God's blessings. He is the source of all good things, including physical rest.

David says He "maketh" me. However, by no means was David implying by force. God is a freewill God. He will not force anyone to do anything they do not want to do. He will not force anyone to receive any blessing they do not want. Instead, the idea the Psalmist is conveying is God lets you experience or takes you to this opportunity. Many translations even use the words "lets" and "takes." However, I like the word "maketh" in this context because it shows our Shepherd's desire. He wills for you to find a place of rest. He tells you that you need to rest.

David then says you will "lie down." The Hebrew word for "lie down" is *rabats* (7257), which means to lie down or stretch out so you can rest. God does not just help you to find a place to lie down, but He wants you to be comfortable. Many come home after work or after a busy day to relax in that familiar, comfortable place. Oftentimes it is some kind of recliner or bed where you can lay back and stretch out your legs so you can get comfortable and rest. You naturally lay down every night to get good sleep. God shows you that He wants you to get the best rest.

The place of rest is in "green" pastures. The Hebrew word for "green" is *deshe* (1877), which means the green grass. It represents flourishing and food for the sheep, the living. The Hebrew word for "pasture" is *naah* (4999), which means pasture, habitation, house, or pleasant place. The place of rest may be your home or a pleasant place you enjoy. It is a physical place that He takes you where He can give your body the rest it needs. One might question and say, "If my house is this place of rest, then I do not need God to lead me there because I can go there." However, this way of thinking is completely wrong because God has to build the house that is peaceful so that you can find nourishment, good rest, and sleep.

> *Except the LORD build the house, they labour in vain that build it: except the LORD keep the city, the watchman waketh but in vain. It is vain for you to rise up early, to sit up late, to eat the bread of sorrows: for so He giveth His beloved sleep.*
>
> —Psalm 127:1–2

There are many homes that were not built by God. In other words, there are homes that are not founded upon the principles of God. Jesus Christ must be the cornerstone of your home. He will then become your Shepherd that takes you to the dwelling place He is in. You will then find that peaceful place you so desperately desire. God can also use a place that is not your home like a retreat or outdoors. The point is God has to be welcomed there.

As a busy minister with a family, I used to feel bad or guilty when I would want to do nothing but rest. It was as if I was not doing the work of the Lord if I was not busy. Furthermore, I had a hard time saying no to anything anyone would ask me because I thought I should always be busy helping others. Obviously, it is good to help others whenever you can, but it is also okay to take care of yourself, because your body is the temple of God's Holy Spirit. When God helped me to understand that it was okay to rest in Him, it changed my life. I recognized that if I want to accomplish everything He has for me, I need to take care of my spirit, soul, and body by physically resting. Many people have requested me for weddings, funerals, and counseling. Since I have an extremely busy schedule,

I have to tell them no almost every time. If I did not, it would lead me to be exhausted and distracted from my true calling. I have learned that just because something may be a good thing does not mean God is calling me to do it. It is God's desire that His children follow His leading and take the time to rest when necessary. Are you physically exhausted and need the Shepherd to lead you to His place of rest? He can give you rest on earth now. Notice that the language of this verse is for those that are alive on earth. Yes, there is physical rest in Heaven in the sense that our body will not tire, not wear down, and not grow old. However, God is willing and wanting to give you rest in Him immediately, and He will feed you along the way. If you are physically tired and struggling to relax, let the Shepherd make your home a godly home so that He can give you rest in your dwelling place. Pray about it. Ask God if there is anything in your home that you need to change or get rid of. Is there something in your dwelling that is ungodly that is hindering rest? It may be movies, pictures, statues, books, figurines, or any number of things that do not please God. Throw them in the trash. Make your habitation a place that God approves of, and welcome God into your dwelling. He will give you that physical rest you are looking for. What a blessing of God!

Pray

"Dear Heavenly Father, I want to accomplish all that You have called me to do. In order for this to happen, I must have a healthy and restful body. Please lead me to the place where I can find Your physical health and rest. Help me to always walk in Your divine health so

that my body will never be lacking in any way. You are the only one that can make my body feel whole and refreshed, and I put my hope and faith in You. May all this be done for Your glory alone. I ask all of this in Jesus' name. Amen."

Declaration of Faith

God, I thank You for giving me Your true physical rest while on earth.

DEVOTIONAL 4

He Leadeth Me Beside the Still Waters

> *He maketh me to lie down in green pastures:* **He leadeth me beside the still waters.**
>
> —Psalm 23:2

There are times in the Bible where God shows His power and might through nature. He made heavy rain fall in Noah's time. He withheld the rain, causing a famine in the land in Joseph's time. He caused a strong east wind to part the Red Sea for Moses and the children of Israel. Nature is under the control of God and is used as He wills and purposes. Psalm 23:2 shows that God also uses nature literally, figuratively, and spiritually. Jesus Christ showed this same idea when He rebuked the wind and spoke to the sea.

> *And He arose, and rebuked the wind, and said unto the sea, Peace, be still. And the wind ceased, and there was a great calm.*
>
> —Mark 4:39

The Lord will calm the storms of life so that you can have His peace. The Shepherd has given you, the sheep, spiritual rest through salvation; you no longer want, and you have physically rested. Now it is time to learn that God leads you to that place of peace.

David will not let you forget that everything begins with "He." The Shepherd is the only one that can be the leader. The Hebrew word for "leadeth" is *nahal* (5095), which means to lead or guide to a watering place or place of rest. It implies a protection. The Hebrew word for "beside" is *al* (5921), which means beside, above, or over. It means going to a place. The Hebrew word for "still" is *menuchah* (4496), which means still, rest, ease, quiet, peacefully, or place of rest. Therefore, this part of verse two could read: He safely guides me to the place of peace.

Many look at the lives of others and see the peace and fulfillment that they so desire for their own lives. God says, "I will not let you see it from afar, but I will let you be familiar with it." Joshua and Caleb saw the promised land and entered into it because they were willing to trust and obey God. As God's sheep, you must trust His willingness to take you to the place of peace because He says He will. You will taste and see the goodness of God in the land of living.

> *O taste and see that the LORD is good: blessed is the man that trusteth in Him.*
>
> —Psalm 34:8

> *I had fainted, unless I had believed to see the goodness of the LORD in the land of the living.*
>
> —Psalm 27:13

The Shepherd knows how to give you the peace and the ease that you need.

God can give peace in multiple ways. He can speak to your heart or supernaturally touch you. He can also give you a literal place of peace. The Hebrew word for "still" is *menuchah* (4496), as mentioned earlier. Notice that one of the definitions stated was place of rest. Your place of peace and ease can sometimes be found in a literal place like your home. Life is busy, and technology with phones and computers is adding to the busyness and noise of life. People are beginning to think that they have to always be seeing something, hearing something, or doing something. It can seem as if there is no off switch for all the noise that goes on around you. God may be saying to go to your prayer closet, prayer room, secret room, secret chamber, or whatever you call this place at your home. This place may be your bedroom, bathroom, or chapel. Shut everything off and be free from distractions. Then seek Him in the stillness because He has the peace.

> *These things I have spoken unto you, that in me ye might have peace. In the world ye shall have tribulation: but be of good cheer; I have overcome the world.*
> —John 16:33

Oftentimes when you are quiet and at rest before Him, you are able to hear His voice.

> *Be still, and know that I am God [...].*
> —Psalm 46:10

Just like God wants to make your home a literal place of physical rest, He wants to make your home a literal place of peace.

Psalm 23:2 ends with the word "waters." The Hebrew word for "waters" is *mayim* (4325), which literally means waters. However, the word waters in the Bible can be literal, figurative, or spiritual. It can be a place where you go and have a peace that comes over you. My family and I enjoy hiking in an area in Ohio called Mohican. There is one particular trail where about a mile and a half in there is a little waterfall. As soon as you arrive at the waterfall, you instantly take it all in. You become relaxed as you gaze at the beautiful sight that God created.

The "waters" that He takes you to can be both figurative and spiritual as Jesus shows.

> *In the last day, that great day of the feast, Jesus stood and cried, saying, If any man thirst, let him come unto Me, and drink. He that believeth on Me, as the scripture hath said, out of his belly shall flow rivers of living water. But this spake He of the Spirit, which they that believe on Him should receive: for the Holy Ghost was not yet given; because that Jesus was not yet glorified.*
>
> —John 7:37–39

Jesus is essentially saying what Psalm 23:2 is saying. He is saying it both in a figurative way and a spiritual way. He is saying, "Come unto Me if you are thirsty for peace and take a drink from Me. I will give you water that will quench you, which is My Spirit that I give you." Notice you have to let Him lead you, then He leads you to His living water, and then He lets you partake through His Spirit.

God leads me to these still waters regularly. He leads me to this place most often by taking me to my prayer closet.

But thou, when thou prayest, enter into thy closet, and when thou hast shut thy door, pray to thy Father which is in secret; and thy Father which seeth in secret shall reward thee openly.

—Matthew 6:6

I look forward to being alone with God. It is not a task, it is not difficult, and it is not burdensome. Rather, it is restful, easy, and a relief. I find myself wanting to spend more and more time with God alone because I am thirsty for Him. Sometimes I will do this multiple times a day because it is such a wonderful time of peaceful fellowship and restoration. If I do not hear from Him right away, I wait on Him because I know He will arrive with His peace.

Do you need the Shepherd's peace in your life? Let Him lead you to that place of still waters. No book can take you there except the Word of God. No person can take you there except the person of the Holy Spirit. It is part of His leading. He knows exactly what you need, how you need it, and how to make sure you receive it. It is a beautiful thing to be led by God into this rest. As the world grows more immoral, as attacks against Christians become more the mainstream, and as we live in the last days before that meeting in the air, it is good to know that our God will give you a peaceful journey in Him on this earth and into eternal life. What a blessing of God!

Pray

"Dear Heavenly Father, You promised that You would lead me to a place where the waters are still. You are the only one that can give me peace in a world where

there are troubles and stress all around me. Please lead me into that place where I can relax and feel refreshed. I want to always have Your peace upon me. May all this be done for Your glory alone. I ask all of this in Jesus' name. Amen."

Declaration of Faith

God, I thank You for always giving me Your peace in every situation.

DEVOTIONAL 5

He Restoreth My Soul

He restoreth my soul: *He leadeth me in the paths of righteousness for His name's sake.*

—Psalm 23:3

I have learned not to settle for anything less than God's perfect will in every area of my life. He has used divine healings, inspiration, wisdom, dreams, visions, knowledge, and so many more great things to accomplish His perfect will in my life. As a minister, I have rightfully focused on God's will in the area of the spirit. God wants to restore a person's spirit to Him through salvation. Through God's abundant grace and power, I have witnessed countless people from all over the world repent, confess, and accept Jesus Christ as their Lord and personal Savior. I have also focused on God's desire to heal the body. I have witnessed God heal a pneumothorax, epilepsy, brain tumors, kidney stones, headaches, lung cancer, broken bones, and numerous other healing miracles. God continues to reveal His will to me and has shown me His desire to restore the soul. The Shepherd has given you, the sheep, spiritual rest through salvation; you no longer want; you have physically rested, and you have peace. Now it is time to learn that God leads you to soul restoration.

Before I show you what restoration means, let's look at this part of verse three backward by looking at what the soul means. God made you to have a spirit, soul, and body, and He cares about every part.

> *And the very God of peace sanctify you wholly; and I pray God your whole spirit and soul and body be preserved blameless unto the coming of our Lord Jesus Christ.*
>
> —1 Thessalonians 5:23

The body is the flesh that houses the spirit and the soul. The body will die by going back to the dust from which it was created (Genesis 3:19) but will someday be made immortal (Philippians 3:21 and 1 Corinthians 15:35–54) to live in Heaven or Hell. The spirit is the part that knows (1 Corinthians 2:11). A Christian's spirit is joined with the Spirit of God that lives inside of the believer (1 Corinthians 6:17). The spirit will always be conscious, so it will never die, so it will continue to live once a person dies, in Heaven or Hell. The Hebrew word for "soul" is *nephesh* (5315), which means soul, that which gives you life or makes you a person. The soul is made up of what you think, feel, and want. Your soul can be called your mind, emotions, and will. It can also be described as your personality. It is the battleground of the flesh and spirit. The soul will never die, so it will continue to live once a person dies, in Heaven or Hell.

David shows at the beginning of this verse that the Shepherd must be the one to bring restoration. There is no one else that can do it. Furthermore, God is specifically concerned with the restoration of our thoughts, our emotional status, and our desires. The Hebrew word for "restoreth" is *shub* (7725), which means to restore, turn back, or return. You may be asking what your soul needs to be restored back to. The answer is simple: godly ways. The restoration that takes place is returning our mind, feelings, and desires back to godly thoughts, emotions, and desires. Remember, the soul is the battleground between our spirit, where God lives, and our flesh.

The devil seeks to damage the soul because He wants to get to your spirit. He does so by trying to get you to think about bad thoughts, by harboring bad feelings and unforgiveness, and by getting our desires to be on things that are ungodly. He also does this by trying to have people say bad things and treat you or your family poorly. If you allow these bad things to take root and you are unrepentant, then it will affect your spirit and walk with God. The devil's ultimate goal is:

> *The thief cometh not, but for to steal, and to kill, and to destroy [...].*
> —John 10:10

Jesus, our Shepherd, has a plan to restore our soul, just as the devil has a plan to destroy it. Look at the second half of John 10:10, "[...] I am come that they might have life, and that they might have it more abundantly."

Notice that Christ's plan is to give you life and to give it to you abundantly. In order to have life abundantly on this earth, you must have your soul in check. You must have a sound mind, stable emotions, and godly desires. Are you frustrated, angry, or sad? Let God restore you. He will take all the bad that the devil has caused in your soul and will return it to good. Christ can do this by showing you how to apply His Word and also by doing it supernaturally.

The Spirit of God will lead you to the right application of His Word in order to teach you how to repair your soul. Philippians 4 is my favorite chapter when it comes to mending your soul because it teaches how to have godly thoughts, feelings, and desires all in one chapter. While I am hesitant to say what verses in this chapter are my favorites because they are all powerful verses, I do have two favorites:

> *Be careful for nothing; but in every thing by prayer and supplication with thanksgiving let your requests be made known unto God. And the peace of God, which passeth all understanding, shall keep your hearts and minds through Christ Jesus.*
>
> —Philippians 4:6–7

I have read those verses and this chapter numerous times when I have had problems with my soul. I have recommended it countless times to help others, and it works.

God has divinely touched my soul many times. I have received this supernatural touch many times while in my prayer closet alone with God. However, I have received it also while driving. I love to drive. If the sun is shining and it is beautiful out, I thoroughly enjoy slowly driving the back roads while praying and enjoying God's beauty. The key to this is that it has to be quiet. Quietness allows you to hear from God so He can bring the restoration you need. Many times in my prayer closet and while driving, God has instantly given my mind peace, calmed my emotions, and changed my desires.

Do you need the Shepherd to restore your soul? Are you feeling great physically but are mentally drained, emotionally exhausted, or having the wrong desires? Just as your body needs rest every night so that it can be ready physically to go where you need to go, your soul needs restoration. Restoration of your soul will help you to feel fresh and ready to take on the challenges of each new day. Let God lead you to that place of restoration because you cannot do it on your own. He alone can help repair your soul by helping you to think about good things, forgive those who have done you wrong, love your enemies, and transform your desires into His desires. If you allow God to be your Shepherd, He will lead you to this place of restoring your soul. What a blessing of God!

Pray

"Dear Heavenly Father, You have given my body rest, and now my soul needs restoration. I cannot think or feel or desire Your ways without Your help. Please lead me into that place where my soul can be repaired so that I may be complete and lacking nothing. Help me to please You always in all I do. May all this be done for Your glory alone. I ask all of this in Jesus' name. Amen."

Declaration of Faith

God, I thank You for always restoring my soul completely.

DEVOTIONAL 6

He Leadeth Me in the Paths of Righteousness

He restoreth my soul: **He leadeth me in the paths of righteousness** *for His name's sake.*

—Psalm 23:3

Growing in the faith is something so important to me. I do not want to just know about God, but I want to know Him personally. I desire to be on the same level of friendship with God that Abraham, Isaac, Jacob, Joseph, Moses, and Joshua were. I want to see the exact miracles happen that I have read about so many times in the Bible. This takes having the fullness of God in my life, and this requires tremendous spiritual growth. I cannot just make myself grow in the faith by doing what I think is right. I am just a sheep, so I need a Shepherd. Yes, I need to do my part, but I really need Him to make my faith grow.

Looking unto Jesus the author and finisher of our faith; who for the joy that was set before Him endured

> *the cross, despising the shame, and is set down at the right hand of the throne of God.*
>
> —Hebrews 12:2

The overflow blessings are reserved for those who know Him in a deeper way.

Many Christians only scratch the surface of God, but God says there is a deeper level to be known about Him.

> *But God hath revealed them unto us by His Spirit: for the Spirit searcheth all things, yea, the deep things of God.*
>
> —1 Corinthians 2:10

The way to the deep things is being led by God down righteous paths. Righteous means right doing. As you learn more about Him, you will become more like Him by growing in the Lord.

> *For therein is the righteousness of God revealed from faith to faith: as it is written, The just shall live by faith.*
>
> —Romans 1:17

He blesses those who act like Him and talk like Him because it is His Word. The Shepherd has given you, the sheep, spiritual rest through salvation; you no longer want; you have physically rested; you have peace, and your soul has been restored. Now it is time to learn that God leads you along righteous paths so that you can experience Him on new levels.

David likes to remind the reader over and over in the first few verses of this psalm how it is "He," as in the Lord, who does everything. Remember, you cannot do anything He has called you to do without Him. Your life would be void of spiritual rest, you would never be satisfied, you would be physically tired, there would be no peace, and your soul would be in discomfort. As soon as you grow in the faith and learn more of God, the devil will tempt you to forget that it was God who accomplished great things in your life. The devil will try to puff you up with pride to become self-righteous. Jesus warns against this:

> *For I say unto you, That except your righteousness shall exceed the righteousness of the scribes and Pharisees, ye shall in no case enter into the kingdom of Heaven.*
> —Matthew 5:20

David was saying that your righteousness must exceed, and the only way it can is by having the Shepherd be the one that leads you.

The Word of God says two verses in a row that He "leadeth." In verse two, He "leadeth" in a guiding and protecting way to the place of peace. The Hebrew word for "leadeth" in this verse is *nachah* (5148), which is slightly different than the Hebrew word in verse two for "leadeth." *Nachah* means to lead or guide but is used in the sense of being led to an unfamiliar place. It is the same Hebrew word used for the word "lead" in:

> *And the LORD went before them by day in a pillar of a cloud, to lead them the way; and by night in a pillar of fire, to give them light; to go by day and night.*
> —Exodus 13:21

The Lord was leading the children of Israel to a place they did not know. Therefore, they could not get to that place on their own. They needed the Lord to guide them to that unfamiliar place. The same idea is presented in this verse of Psalm 23. The paths of righteousness are not a place you know. It is an unfamiliar place because you have no righteousness outside of Jesus Christ.

> *But we are all as an unclean thing, and all our righteousnesses are as filthy rags; and we all do fade as a leaf; and all our iniquities, like the wind, have taken us away.*
>
> —Isaiah 64:6

It is the righteousness of God that covers your sin and makes you right with Him. It is the perfect sacrifice of the blood of Jesus Christ that makes you able to say you are righteous. God leads you in the paths of righteousness, and without Him, you would be lost because you do not know the way. We need God to help us to go down the right paths of righteousness in every area of our lives.

The Hebrew word for "paths" is *magal* (4570), which means paths, track, or entrenchment. Notice that it is a track or a path. It is not a big, vast, or wide road. The paths are straight and narrow, and not many have traveled them.

> *Enter ye in at the strait gate: for wide is the gate, and broad is the way, that leadeth to destruction, and many there be which go in thereat: Because strait is the gate, and narrow is the way, which leadeth unto life, and few there be that find it.*
>
> —Matthew 7:13–14

The Psalmist is by *no* means suggesting there is more than one way to Heaven by choosing the word "paths." There is clearly only one path to Heaven, and that is through Jesus Christ.

> *Jesus saith unto him, "I am the way, the truth, and the life: no man cometh unto the Father, but by me."*
> —John 14:6

Instead, the Psalmist is saying there will be many questions, problems, and situations arising in your life, but God knows the "paths" that you need to take concerning every area of your life.

All of the Shepherd's leadings are paths of righteousness. The Hebrew word for "righteousness" is *tsedeq* (6664), which means, righteousness, to be right, or to do right. Everything God does is always correct and righteous because He is righteous.

> *For the righteous LORD loveth righteousness; His countenance doth behold the upright.*
> —Psalm 11:7

Jesus had no sin because He is righteous.

> *And ye know that He was manifested to take away our sins; and in Him is no sin.*
> —1 John 3:5

Jesus says that the Holy Spirit convicts people of sin, shows that people's righteousness alone is no good, and tells how Jesus alone is the only way to be saved. The Holy Spirit does this because He is righteous.

> *And when He is come, He will reprove the world of sin, and of righteousness, and of judgment.*
>
> —John 16:8

I have been blessed with a God-given, growing, worldwide ministry that includes television, radio, social media, and books. The inquiries and questions I receive, along with the decisions that I have to make, number in the tens of thousands. Add to all of this the fact that I want to handle everything in a way that is God's perfect will; decision-making could become overwhelming. But it is not. It is not hard, difficult, or overwhelming because I have discovered the secret: if I let the Lord lead me, He will take me down the correct path for every inquiry, every question, and every decision that I have to make.

Many times I have found the answers as to which paths to take during my praying and seeking of God while in my prayer closet. The Bible shows what to do during this time for the Shepherd to lead you.

Romans 12:1–2 says,

> *I beseech you therefore, brethren, by the mercies of God, that ye present your bodies a living sacrifice, holy, acceptable unto God, which is your reasonable service. And be not conformed to this world: but be ye transformed by the renewing of your mind, that ye may prove what is that good, and acceptable, and perfect will of God.*

I do what Romans 12:1–2 says to do while praying about the situations in front of me, and I let God lead me. Obviously, I cannot always pray about every request, every question, and every decision because that would be physically impossible.

Therefore, I also let God lead me in His paths of righteousness by letting His peace lead me into what is His will and what is not His will.

> *And let the peace of God rule in your hearts, to the which also ye are called in one body; and be ye thankful.*
>
> —Colossians 3:15

The Greek word for "rule" in that verse is *brabeuo* (1018), which means to rule or arbitrate. An arbitrator is like an umpire or ref in a sporting event. For example, in a game of baseball, an arbitrator or umpire would call balls and strikes behind home plate. The umpire would call what is safe and out. The peace of God is to call what is safe and out. God can lead you on paths of righteousness by whether or not He gives you peace about a situation, question, problem, and every other area in life. Therefore, let the peace of God rule you.

Are you facing multiple decisions in life where you need the Shepherd to tell you what to do? The good news is that He will lead you. He will take you down the right paths, which you could not figure out on your own. You have to spend time with Him through prayer, reading His Word, and going to church. You have to listen carefully to the Spirit of God because He speaks through peace. The Shepherd loves you. If you follow Him, His righteous paths lead to the blessings of God.

> *For thou, LORD, wilt bless the righteous; with favour wilt thou compass him as with a shield.*
>
> —Psalm 5:12

The Lord will lead you down His righteous paths to His blessings. What a blessing of God!

Pray

"Dear Heavenly Father, You alone are righteous. Please cover me with Your righteousness. May I always sit, walk, and run in the paths that You would have me to go down. I ask for Your wisdom concerning every area of my life. May all this be done for Your glory alone. I ask all of this in Jesus' name. Amen."

Declaration of Faith

God, I thank You for leading me and giving me the strength to follow You in Your righteous paths.

DEVOTIONAL 7

For His Name's Sake

> *He restoreth my soul: He leadeth me in the paths of righteousness* **for His name's sake***.*
>
> —Psalm 23:3

I have been blessed to preach the gospel for over twenty years. During these years, I have been asked about every question imaginable. Some of them are funny, some are sad, and some are very serious. One question that always touches my heart is, "Why did God create me?" Usually, when someone asks me this question, they are really struggling spiritually and in their soul. I am sure there are millions and millions of people around the world who are asking themselves the same question. Psalm 23:3 answers that very question. The Shepherd has given you, the sheep, spiritual rest through salvation; you no longer want; you have physically rested; you have peace; your soul has been restored, and you are on righteous paths. Now it is time to learn that God leads you to fulfill the purpose of your existence.

To understand the reason for your creation, you need to go back to the beginning. God created everything (Genesis 1:1). He created the angel Lucifer who then rebelled, was kicked out of Heaven to earth, and became the devil (Ezekiel

28:14–19). God created Adam and Eve and gave them power and dominion over His earth (Genesis 1:26–31). Adam and Eve sinned and gave dominion back to the devil (Genesis 3). Jesus Christ will return soon to take back power and set up His eternal kingdom to live with all His people throughout eternal life (Revelation 11:15).

Let me go back to Genesis 1, where God first created mankind. Did God need Adam and Eve? No! God did not need Adam and Eve to become complete or to feel whole or satisfied. He is God. I do not complete God. You do not complete God. He is already perfect. Why would God create someone then in His image as He did in Genesis 1:26? The Hebrew word for "image" is *tselem* (6754), which means image as in a resemblance in regards to an outward form. This means you have outward features as God also has outward features. God wanted a family that looked like Him and acted like Him. He wanted to have fellowship with His creation as shown by Him walking in the cool of the day to talk with His son and daughter (Genesis 3:8). God chose to make you but for what purpose?

God made you with a purpose. He has a plan for you and everyone else that He has created. His plan is simple: that you glorify God. The purpose of your existence is to bring God glory. You were created with His glory in mind.

> *Even every one that that is called by my name: for I have created him for My glory, I have formed him; yea, I have made him.*
>
> —Isaiah 43:7

Though the specific ways He uses you to bring Him glory are unique to every individual, everyone should bring Him glory in everything they do.

> *Whether therefore ye eat, or drink, or whatsoever ye do, do all to the glory of God.*
> —1 Corinthians 10:31

As the Lord directs your steps down His paths of righteousness, it is so you can be used to bring glory to Him.

Psalm 23:3 is teaching you the principle that you cannot glorify God if He is not leading you. In other words, you cannot fulfill your purpose without Him. You will be a lost sheep wandering aimlessly, trying to figure out your life on your own. The Hebrew word for "name" in this verse is *shem* (8034), which means having a reflection on someone or their reputation or fame. The Hebrew word for "sake" is *maan* (4616), which means sake, purpose, or intent. Therefore, you are led down correct paths for God's fame and purpose. Wow! Process that for a moment: the God who created everything wants to use you to bring Him glory. He cares about you.

Make no mistake about it: God is concerned with His reputation, and He does not want the devil to receive glory. One of my favorite Bible stories is found in Numbers 14. God had enough of the murmuring of the children of Israel, so He was going to destroy them. He said He would start over with a new group with Moses still as His chosen leader. However, Moses interceded by praying and telling God that if He destroyed them, then the nations would say how He was not able to bring them into the land He promised them. In essence, Moses was saying that God would not be glorified, but instead, His enemies would win. God understands that there are only two options: glorify God or glorify the devil. God heard Moses' request and spared the people so that He would receive the glory, and then He made a beautiful statement:

> *But as truly as I live, all the earth shall be filled with the glory of the LORD.*
>
> —Numbers 14:21

You are a direct reflection of Him because He puts His name on you by calling you a Christian. You are the seed of Abraham, His family, and joint-heirs with Christ. You are made in His image. Does it glorify God if you are depressed, harbor resentment, have condemnation, are sick, financially struggling, or have a problem? The answer to that question can be found by answering this question: are you happy when your children are experiencing something bad? *No!* Neither does God get joy out of seeing His children barely making it in life. God's plan is to bless you spiritually, physically, mentally, emotionally, relationally, and financially. He desires this so that you might bring glory to Him by praising Him and telling others about God's goodness.

I am convinced that it is God's will to bless me so that I can turn and bless Him. He created me for it. I was recently prayerfully mediating on the scripture:

> *Now unto Him that is able to do exceeding abundantly above all that we ask or think, according to the power that worketh in us.*
>
> —Ephesians 3:20

What a beautiful promise of God. He is able and willing to do more than I could have ever imagined or dreamt. I am a living example of this scripture. I could have never imagined how He would open doors for me to preach all around the world. Why did He bless me like this? The answer is simple: that I might glorify Him. His glory alone is my focus in life, and because of that, I am being led to where the blessings of God continue to chase me down.

> *And all these blessings shall come on thee, and overtake thee, if thou shalt hearken unto the voice of the LORD thy God.*
> —Deuteronomy 28:2

Are you being used by the Shepherd to bring Him glory? Let Him lead you into the correct paths so that His mission can be accomplished. You will experience God's blessings as a result. Spend time with Him alone, and do not try to figure out how you can glorify God. Instead, ask Him to direct your paths to bring glory to His name in all you do.

> *Trust in the LORD with all thine heart; and lean not unto thine own understanding. In all thy ways acknowledge Him, and He shall direct thy paths.*
> —Proverbs 3:5–6

God will use you greatly to glorify Him. What a blessing of God!

Pray

"Dear Heavenly Father, I want to glorify You in all I do. Please lead me down Your righteous paths that I may accomplish all that You would desire for me to do. Bless me indeed to honor You. May all this be done

for Your glory alone. I ask all of this in Jesus' name. Amen."

Declaration of Faith

God, I thank You for using me to bring great glory to Your name over all the earth.

DEVOTIONAL 8

Yea, Though I Walk through the Valley of the Shadow of Death

Yea, though I walk through the valley of the shadow of death, *I will fear no evil: for Thou art with me; Thy rod and Thy staff they comfort me.*

—Psalm 23:4

The first three verses of Psalm 23 bring to mind a beautiful picture of sheep being led to wonderful places by the Good Shepherd. Upon reading verse four, it seems to paint a different picture than the first three verses because it uses the harsh word "death." Death is a subject that no one likes to talk about. People feel uncomfortable thinking about their own mortality, so most people just avoid the subject altogether. As a minister and senior pastor, I am acquainted with death and tragedy. I have done countless funerals for all age groups. God has given me the strength, ability, and wisdom to deal with families during times of grief. God has shown me through all these dealings that Psalm 23 is not for the dead, but it is for the living.

Many think this verse is talking about the death of loved ones. However, that is not what this verse is saying. This verse is saying that it is a "shadow," so this has to be understood in literal, figurative, and spiritual context. Therefore, it is not actual death the sheep experiences but something the living goes through, which I will explain in more detail shortly. The Shepherd has given you, the sheep, spiritual rest through salvation; you no longer want; you have physically rested; you have peace; your soul has been restored; you are on righteous paths, and you glorify God. Now it is time to learn that God leads you through the "shadow of death."

Verse four opens up saying "Yea," and the Hebrew word for this is *gam* (1571), which means yeah, moreover, or also. The Psalmist acknowledges that everything he has been led to so far has been great, but he is certain that he is going to face evil. He expresses this with that little Hebrew word *gam*. He is in essence saying, "Yeah, it will happen," "Even when it happens," or "I know it will happen." The Psalmist knows that when you are trying to live a life walking with God, the devil will rear his ugly head. Paul noticed the same thing in his life.

> *I find then a law, that, when I would do good, evil is present with me.*
>
> —Romans 7:21

If you have been a Christian long enough and have been trying your best to live for Him, you know how the devil works on you. He attacks you spiritually, physically, mentally, emotionally, relationally, and financially. Thankfully, the Shepherd knows how to lead you during these dark times.

You will walk through dark times, the Psalmist says. The Hebrew word for "walk" is *halak* (1980), which means to walk, to come, or to go. The Hebrew word for "valley" is *gay* (1516), which means valley. However, it carries with it the idea of a low place that is scary. The Hebrew word for "shadow of death" is *tsalmaveth* (6757), which means a deep shadow that is death-like. In summary of the verse so far: yeah, you will travel through scary places where it looks like death is upon you. However, remember, it is not actual death. The Shepherd is not going to let you die until you have completed the work He has for you. These shadows of death are just a mirage to try and bring fear upon you.

This "shadow of death" place you will travel to can have a literal meaning, like you are going to die physically. In other words, this evil presents itself like a physical death is going to happen. You may find this place to be a difficult time in your life dealing with a health scare or terminal diagnosis, a near-death experience like a car accident, or a death threat from a person or group. The good news is the Shepherd does not let you physically die. I have experienced almost all of these "shadow of death" examples. I was in a car accident when I was fifteen, and they did not know if I was going to live or not, which is when I repented, confessed, and accepted Jesus Christ as my Lord and personal Savior. I have had people try to attack me, have been threatened to be killed twice, and once had a gun pulled on me. About ten years ago, for almost one year straight, I had severe headaches every day. I was checked twice for brain tumors, but thankfully, there were none, and God healed me of headaches. Glory be to God because He has been with me in all of these situations and led me through them all.

This "shadow of death" place you will travel to can have a figurative meaning because death is represented in a loss. You may find this place to be a difficult time in your life, like a loss of a marriage (divorce), loss of a job, or loss of a loved one. The good news is the Shepherd does not let this loss destroy you. I have experienced some of these "shadow of death" examples. I was four years old when my parents divorced, and it resulted in me having some difficult and depressing times in my childhood. When I was a younger minister, I also had a job with the United States Post Office, and the government cut my position, so I lost my job. My wife and I had just bought a home and had our eldest son Ricky. I remember thinking, *How are we going to make it financially*. I have lost many people in my life that are near and dear to me, like my grandparents, who were like parents to me, and a younger brother. Glory be to God, though, because He was with me in all of these situations and led me through them all.

This "shadow of death" place you will travel to can have a spiritual meaning because death appears to have happened in your spiritual walk with God. You may find this place to be a difficult time in your walk with God where you have not heard from God in a while, felt His presence, or seen His hand move in your life. It may seem like a "dry" season spiritually, and the devil is attacking you over and over, trying to get you to question the existence of your faith. The good news is the Shepherd does not allow you to become lost. I have experienced these "shadow of death" examples. I have wondered where God was. I have prayed and prayed and prayed, but nothing seemed to happen. During these times, the devil has tried to devour me. I have learned to remember that during these times, God is with me and that I need to live by faith.

> *Let your conversation be without covetousness; and be content with such things as ye have: for He hath said, I will never leave thee, nor forsake thee.*
> —Hebrews 13:5

> *Now the just shall live by faith: but if any man draw back, My soul shall have no pleasure in Him.*
> —Hebrews 10:38

Glory be to God, though, because He was with me in all of these situations and led me through them all.

David did not experience death during any of his difficult times, even though he was a man of war. He only experienced the shadows of death. Goliath could not kill him, Saul could not kill him, and Absalom could not kill him. He fought battle after battle physically and spiritually. He continued to remain steadfast in the knowledge that every evil thing he faced was merely a shadow. He knew he would only experience death when God was ready to take him.

Are you facing a difficult situation where you need the Shepherd to stop the devouring lion from destroying you? If not now, you eventually will.

> *Be sober, be vigilant; because your adversary the devil, as a roaring lion, walketh about, seeking whom he may devour.*
> —1 Peter 5:8

The Greek word in this scripture for "walketh" is *peripateo* (4043), which means to walk, prowl around, or follow. Notice that you are walking as sheep, as the Spirit of God is leading you, and the devil is walking like a lion following you. The devil will attack and will try to devour you if you let him. However, you do not have to worry. You are with the Good Shepherd. He loves you, and He cares for you. He has the power to protect you.

> *Ye are of God, little children, and have overcome them: because greater is He that is in you, than he that is in the world.*
>
> —1 John 4:4

You will see these shadows of death at various points in your life. Take comfort because you will not experience death until God is ready to call you home. You will not experience destruction. You will not become lost. Do not give in to fear. Evil will not prevail! What a blessing of God!

Pray

> *"Dear Heavenly Father, help me to live by Your faith during times when the shadows of death are around me. Please dispel every demon and the devil that comes and tries to bring evil against my family and me. I bind and rebuke every evil spirit and command them to leave in Jesus' name. May all this be done for Your glory alone. I ask all of this in Jesus' name. Amen."*

Declaration of Faith

God, I thank You for protecting my family and me when evil tries to attack.

DEVOTIONAL 9

I Will Fear No Evil

> *Yea, though I walk through the valley of the shadow of death,* **I will fear no evil**: *for Thou art with me; Thy rod and Thy staff they comfort me.*
>
> —Psalm 23:4

My wife, Victoria, and I are blessed to have three wonderful God-fearing kids: Ricky, Riley, and Vera. As parents, we have taught our kids to fear the basic things that most parents teach their kids to fear: watch for vehicles when crossing the road, do not talk to strangers, and be careful when swimming. Parents are right to teach their children to have a healthy fear of these things and other dangers. We have also taught our kids what it means to have the "fear of the LORD" (Proverbs 1:7), which means to have a reverential respect for the Lord and His power. Jesus says it is important to fear God.

> *And fear not them which kill the body, but are not able to kill the soul: but rather fear Him which is able to destroy both soul and body in Hell.*
>
> —Matthew 10:28

We feel satisfied knowing we have taught our children to fear the right things. It is also our job to teach our kids what not to fear. They should not fear any kind of evil. Why? Because the Bible says so. That settles it. The Shepherd has given you, the sheep, spiritual rest through salvation; you no longer want; you have physically rested; you have peace; your soul has been restored; you are on righteous paths; you glorify God, and evil has not prevailed against you. Now it is time to learn that God leads you to no longer fear.

The Psalmist makes a strong declaration against fear by saying, "I will fear no evil." The Hebrew word for "fear" is *yare* (3372), which means to fear or frighten. The Hebrew word for "no" is *lo* (3808), which simply means no. The Hebrew word for "evil" is *ra*, which means evil or bad. David is clearly saying that he will not be frightened by anything bad. Wow, what a statement! Can you say this? Can you say that you do not care what happens around you or what the circumstances look like because you will not fear?

David is able to say that he has no fear despite the evil around him. David tells Saul how he killed a lion and bear, so he is not afraid of Goliath.

> *And David said unto Saul, Thy servant kept his father's sheep, and there came a lion, and a bear, and took a lamb out of the flock: And I went out after him, and smote him, and delivered it out of his mouth: and when he arose against me, I caught him by his beard, and smote him, and slew him. Thy servant slew both the lion and the bear: and this uncircumcised Philistine shall be as one of them, seeing he hath defiled the armies of the living God.*
>
> —1 Samuel 17:34–36

Just like God helped David to have no fear, He wants to do the same for you.

The devil tries to bring fear upon you when everything seems to be going great. God has saved you and led you to so many blessings in life. Maybe He has blessed you with the perfect spouse, given you great kids, a nice home, and a job you enjoy. You have His fruit of the Spirit in your life. (You may be saying that you have not experienced anything good yet in your life. Please reread Devotional Messages One and Two because they will help start your journey to the paths of God's blessings.) All of a sudden, the devil, that voracious lion, comes and tries to cause divorce, tries to get your kids on the wrong paths, tries to cause financial problems, and tries to get your co-workers to hate you. The devil tries to steal your love, joy, and peace. Everything looks bad because that "shadow of death" is around you. As a sheep, you could become tense and fearful knowing that any of these things could destroy you. However, you know the Shepherd personally, so you do not have to fear. He has taken care of you this far, so you are not going to fear. You can look at the devil and his demons, and you do not even flinch. Why? Your Shepherd, the Lord God, has power over the devil and the demons, so there is no reason to fear.

> *And He healed many that were sick of divers diseases, and cast out many devils; and suffered not the devils to speak, because they knew Him.*
> —Mark 1:34

The Lord will take away your fear.

I would be lying if I said that I never had fear when I experienced the shadows of death or evil things. It is hard not to be in the flesh and be without fear when someone tries to attack you, threatens to kill you, and when a gun is pulled on you.

However, I know that God wants to get all His children to the point of having no fear despite all of the evil around them. In the next devotional message, you will learn that you should not fear because He is always with you. There are many other aspects of God that have helped me not to fear, but I will share three of them with you: He is good, He is faithful, and He has all power. God is good, which is why Jesus is called the "Good Shepherd." He will always be good to you.

> *For the LORD is good; His mercy is everlasting; and His truth endureth to all generations.*
>
> —Psalm 100:5

> *I am the Good Shepherd: the Good Shepherd giveth His life for the sheep.*
>
> —John 10:11

He is faithful, and so is His Word. He will always come through and fulfill His Word.

> *But the Lord is faithful, who shall stablish you, and keep you from evil.*
>
> —2 Thessalonians 3:3

> *So shall my Word be that goeth forth out of my mouth: it shall not return unto me void, but it shall accomplish that which I please, and it shall prosper in the thing whereto I sent it.*
>
> —Isaiah 55:11

He has all power. He will always protect you with His power.

And Jesus came and spake unto them, saying, "All power is given unto me in Heaven and in earth."
—Matthew 28:18

And He hath on His vesture and on His thigh a name written, King of kings, and Lord of lords.
—Revelation 19:16

Remembering that the Lord is good, faithful, and that He has all power will help you not to give in to the spirit of fear.

Do you need the Good Shepherd to remove the fear that has come upon you? It is time you put your trust in God. He does not want anything to happen to you because He is a good God. He leads to good places. He is faithful and will come through for you. Furthermore, He can make all the evil disappear immediately because of His power. God can help you get to the point in your life where you can say, "I will fear no evil." What a blessing of God!

Pray

"Dear Heavenly Father, help me to never have fear. Remind me of Your goodness, faithfulness, and power. Please help me to boldly stand in the face of evil and declare that You will take care of me always. I bind and rebuke every evil spirit and command them to leave in Jesus' name. May all this be done for Your glory alone. I ask all of this in Jesus' name. Amen."

Declaration of Faith

God, I thank You for helping me to never fear anyone or anything but You.

DEVOTIONAL 10

For Thou Art with Me

Yea, though I walk through the valley of the shadow of death, I will fear no evil: **for Thou art with me;** *Thy rod and Thy staff they comfort me.*
—Psalm 23:4

God could have chosen to hide Himself from His creation. He could have chosen to make it where people have knowledge of Him but never experience Him. The good news is that He did not choose to do either one of those things. Instead, He chose to reveal Himself to His creation through the revelation of His Word and the Holy Spirit. Therefore, you can know God's attributes, you can know His likes, and you can know His dislikes. God wants you to know about Him and wants you to have a close fellowship with Him. How do I know that? Because He makes you His family. That is right, He is your Father, and you are His child. You are adopted into His family through salvation in Jesus Christ.

For ye are all the children of God by faith in Christ Jesus.
—Galatians 3:26

God walked with His first family members, Adam and Eve, in the cool of the day showing His desire to be a part of their lives:

> *And they heard the voice of the LORD God walking in the garden in the cool of the day: Adam and his wife hid themselves from the presence of the LORD God amongst the trees of the garden.*
>
> —Genesis 3:8

The Shepherd has given you, the sheep, spiritual rest through salvation; you no longer want; you have physically rested; you have peace; your soul has been restored; you are on righteous paths; you glorify God; evil has not prevailed against you, and you do not fear. Now it is time to learn that God leads you to realize He is always with you.

You have learned that you should not fear because our Shepherd is good, faithful, and all-powerful. Now it is also time to learn not to fear because He is always with you. Evil is around you constantly, but where is God during these difficult times? The Psalmist answers this question in this part of the verse by boldly declaring He is with you. The Hebrew word used for the phrase "art with me" is *immad* (5978), which means art with me, against, by, or mine. The Hebrew is literally saying that the Lord is by you. Just because times got tough and bad things have happened does not mean that God left you. The Shepherd does not abandon His sheep.

The Bible shows in the Old Testament passages that God is with you wherever you are at. Even when you do not think He is with you, He is with you from the womb, while on earth, and in eternal life.

> *Whither shall I go from thy spirit? or whither shall I flee from thy presence? If I ascend up into Heaven, thou art there: if I make my bed in Hell, behold, thou art there. If I take the wings of the morning, and dwell in the uttermost parts of the sea; Even there shall thy hand lead me, and thy right hand shall hold me. If I say, Surely the darkness shall cover me; even the night shall be light about me. Yea, the darkness hideth not from thee; but the night shineth as the day: the darkness and the light are both alike to thee. For thou hast possessed my reins: thou hast covered me in my mother's womb.*
>
> —Psalm 139:7–12

The Hebrew word for "presence" in verse seven is *pamim* (6440), which means presence or face. It is a plural word indicating more than one face, which shows the Trinity: God the Father, God the Son, and God the Holy Spirit. In other words, the Trinity is with you.

The Bible shows in the New Testament that God is with you through Jesus.

> *Behold, a virgin shall be with child, and shall bring forth a son, and they shall call His name Emmanuel, which being interpreted is, God with us.*
>
> —Matthew 1:23

The Holy Spirit is with you also by living inside of the believer.

> *Know ye not that ye are the temple of God, and that the Spirit of God dwelleth in you?*
>
> —1 Corinthians 3:16

By now, you understand that the Trinity is with you. You can turn your back on God, but He will never turn His back on you.

While I have experienced numerous "shadow of death" experiences, from a young age, I have always known that God was with me. One time when I was younger, I was riding my bike and praying while asking God where He was. I had not seen His hand or experienced Him recently, so I was questioning Him. About that time, I passed a church that had on their sign, "I haven't gone anywhere, but where have you gone? *God.*" The Holy Spirit used that to speak to my heart. From that day forward, I have been blessed with a peace of knowing that God is always with me.

God wants people to understand, especially in hard times, that He is with them. One night I was called over to a family's house because their twenty-one-year-old severely handicapped daughter was dying. She was only expected to live until she was two, but by the grace of God, she had made it far past that. As she lay there dying, her mom was sobbing and asked me a question, something like, "What should I do?" Immediately, the Spirit of the Lord spoke to me to tell her that He was right there with her and that He would be her strength. On another occasion, I went to visit a man who had Parkinson's disease and was physically and mentally struggling. God kept telling me to tell him that He was there with him.

Are you experiencing the "shadow of death" around you and wondering where the Shepherd is? I tell you the same thing I said to that mom and that man: God is right there with you. He has not left you because, after all, He promises to stay with you.

Be strong and of a good courage, fear not, nor be afraid of them: for the LORD thy God, He it is that doth go with thee; He will not fail thee, nor forsake thee.

—Deuteronomy 31:6

Be encouraged through His Word and His Spirit that God is always with you. What a blessing of God!

Pray

"Dear Heavenly Father, help me to always remember that You are with me. Even when the devil tries to convince me otherwise by surrounding me with evil on every side, I call out to You in faith. May all this be done for Your glory alone. I ask all of this in Jesus' name. Amen."

Declaration of Faith

God, I thank You for helping me to know that You are always with me.

DEVOTIONAL 11

Thy Rod and Thy Staff

Yea, though I walk through the valley of the shadow of death, I will fear no evil: for Thou art with me; **Thy rod and Thy staff** *they comfort me.*

—Psalm 23:4

As a pastor/shepherd of a church and having numerous ministry partners, it is my God-given responsibility to take care of them in a defensive and protective way. I do my best to keep the devil and his demons from hurting my sheep spiritually, physically, mentally, emotionally, relationally, and financially. I use the Word of God as a rod and staff. I preach, teach, and help them grow in the faith as the Spirit of God leads me. I defend and protect them by teaching them about how the kingdom of darkness works and how to stand up in the power of God.

> *For we wrestle not against flesh and blood, but against principalities, against powers, against the rulers of the darkness of this world, against spiritual wickedness in high places. Wherefore take unto you the*

> *whole armour of God that ye may be able to withstand in the evil day, and having done all, to stand.*
> —Ephesians 6:12–13

I have taught them that when people treat you badly, it is the result of that person's bad decision(s), but the devil is behind it. Therefore, I defend them by praying for them and with them. I also defend them by rebuking the devil and his demons and commanding them to leave in the powerful name of Jesus Christ.

I protect my sheep also by gently correcting and directing them. There is a fine line between how, when, and where to correct someone. Correction is sometimes necessary because it protects the sheep spiritually and in many other ways. The best advice to any pastor or spiritual leader in a situation where correction is needed is to pray about it and ask for God's wisdom and leading. God may have you correct them immediately, or He may have you wait because sometimes you have to catch the fish before you can clean the fish. I first became a senior pastor at the age of twenty-four, and within the first few months of my pastoring, I noticed a problem that was affecting my church. A lady from our church was causing a ruckus regularly because a young boy, about fifteen years old, was wearing knee-length cargo shorts while playing the guitar during our worship service. She did not like him wearing shorts at all. Every Sunday, she was telling me how I was wrong for allowing it. I prayed and prayed but did not know what to do. I did not want to run this kid and his family out of church for something as petty as that, but I also did not want to have this woman continuing to chirp in my ear, so I prayed about it.

After much praying, I received an answer from God. He told me to tell her that we were going to love that boy and his family and that he was not doing anything wrong or immodest. I told her she could come to the board and voice her complaint if she would like. She was not happy. She left and took several with her. At the time, it was devastating, but God told me that for every person that left, He would send three in their place, and He did. The good news is that we did not run a boy and his family out of church; the lady that left found another church. The lady and I would see each other at church events, and we were always cordial. Years later, I was led by God to visit her in the nursing home, and we prayed together. Then, the next day, she died. She was right and ready with God, glory to His name. The Shepherd has given you, the sheep, spiritual rest through salvation; you no longer want; you have physically rested; you have peace; your soul has been restored; you are on righteous paths; you glorify God; evil has not prevailed against you; you do not fear, and He is always with you. Now it is time to learn that God leads you with His defense and protection.

David proclaims God's defense and protection when he says "Thy rod and Thy staff." The rod defends from the enemy while the staff protects the sheep oftentimes from themselves. God defends and protects you because He loves you. The Hebrew word for "rod" is *shebet* (7626), which means rod, staff, or club. The rod was used by shepherds to defend their sheep from predators. It was a shorter and heavier club that could be used to strike anything and anyone that came against their sheep. In modern terms, it could be called a weapon for self-defense. The rod was probably used by David when he killed the lion and bear (1 Samuel 17:34–36). The rod was also used to count sheep (Leviticus 17:32).

The staff is just as necessary for the sheep's protection. The Hebrew word for "staff" is *mish'enah* (4938), which means a staff, support, sustenance, or walking stick. The staff was used to protect the sheep from themselves, so it, in essence, supported and helped maintain the life of the sheep. It was a longer stick with a hook at one end. This kind of stick became known as a shepherd's crook. If the sheep would wander off the path or become trapped, the shepherd could save the sheep by using the hook to bring them back to him. The staff keeps the sheep close to the shepherd.

I have seen my Shepherd, God Almighty, use His rod against my enemies in order to defend me. My enemy is the devil, but sometimes people allow the devil to use them as his tools. If people allow the devil to use them against God's sheep and they do not repent, watch out because the Shepherd will use His rod as a weapon. God defends His anointed.

> *Saying, Touch not mine anointed, and do my prophets no harm.*
>
> —Psalm 105:15

I could share countless examples of God coming to my rescue. For now, I will give you one example. One time I was ministering at a church as a guest, and the microphone was a little loud for that small church. About three minutes into my preaching, I asked the audio person if he would turn down the microphone, which he did with no problem. Immediately after that, a gentleman from the guest band that was also there that night stood up in the church and began to berate me in front of the congregation. He called me stupid along with other things for not turning it down sooner. I took the high road and apologized, even though it was not my fault at all. The pastor of the church said nothing about the incident, so I went back to preaching. After I was done, I went up to that gentleman and that band to try and apologize again for the microphone being too loud, just to be nice and loving. Every member in the band purposely ignored me and would not speak to me. I knew they were allowing the devil to use them, and the way they were coming against me was not of God. I left there having the most awful experience ever as a guest preacher. God even told me that I would never have to go back there.

Less than six months later, the leader of that band died unexpectedly, the pastor's adult grandson died unexpectedly, and several others from that church died unexpectedly, all within months. Someone from the church called me and asked me to pray for the church, which I did. This story may sound like God is harsh, but God is not. God is actually extremely merciful and gracious. However, do not mess with His children and remain unrepentant.

> *The LORD is merciful and gracious, slow to anger, and plenteous in mercy.*
> —Psalm 103:8

God allows people to make choices, and if they choose badly (sin), then they need to know that bad things will happen if they continue to sin and do not repent.

> *Be not deceived; God is not mocked: for whatsoever a man soweth, that shall he also reap.*
> —Galatians 6:7

Eventually, sin will bring death.

> *For the wages of sin is death; but the gift of God is eternal life through Jesus Christ our Lord.*
>
> —Romans 6:23

God does not want or cause bad things to happen. God is only a good God. The devil wants and causes bad things to happen. The devil is only bad. Jesus shows this in His Word.

> *The thief cometh not, but for to steal, and to kill, and to destroy: I am come that they might have life, and that they might have it more abundantly.*
>
> —John 10:10

God is desperately trying to get people to accept His love, forgiveness, and the life He offers. I do not know all the sins of that band or that church. I do not know what bad things they might have said about me. However, I do know that they "touched" me, and I am His anointed, were unrepentant, and God's hedge of protection was removed from them. Once God's protection was removed, the roaring lion (devil) devoured those that remained in sin. I caution everyone: if you do not like some preacher, that is fine, but do not run your mouth about them. Instead, pray for them.

I have been blessed to remain serious and faithful to God since the age of fifteen. However, that does not mean that there were not times in my life when God had to get His staff of protection out in order to protect me from wandering down the wrong path. The wrong path is anything outside the will of God. I have had people approach me over the years asking me to become their pastor or become the director of their ministry. Thankfully, in the Shepherd's protection, He took His hook and pulled me back, saying, "Not that way, but this way." God knows how to close doors just as well as He knows how to open doors.

Are you in a situation where you need the Shepherd to defend or protect you? God will fight the enemy, the devil, by beating him with His rod. No weapon formed against you will prevail when God is with you.

> *No weapon that is formed against thee shall prosper; and every tongue that shall rise against thee in judgment thou shalt condemn. This is the heritage of the servants of the LORD, and their righteousness is of me, saith the LORD.*
>
> —Isaiah 54:17

Follow God and bind, rebuke, and command the devil and his demons to leave in Jesus name.

> *Submit yourselves therefore to God. Resist the devil, and he will flee from you.*
>
> —James 4:7

God will protect you by using His staff to lovingly correct you.

> *For whom the LORD loveth He correcteth; even as a father the son in whom he delighteth.*
>
> —Proverbs 3:12

In the next devotional message, you will learn that God's defense and protection comfort you. For now, know that God defends and protects you because He loves you. What a blessing of God!

Pray

"Dear Heavenly Father, help me to always remember that You will defend and protect me in the good times and in the bad. Please help me to know that the devil will not prevail against me because You are greater than anything and anyone. May all this be done for Your glory alone. I ask all of this in Jesus' name. Amen."

Declaration of Faith

God, I thank You for defending and protecting me everywhere I go.

DEVOTIONAL 12

They Comfort Me

> *Yea, though I walk through the valley of the shadow of death, I will fear no evil: for Thou art with me; Thy rod and Thy staff* **they comfort me.**
>
> —Psalm 23:4

The need for comfort is a basic human need that all share. Comfort is ease from pain and feelings of distress. Compassion, which is pity and concern, is what causes someone to want to comfort another. The world is in desperate need of comfort after dealing with the pestilence of Covid, the wars and rumors of war in Europe and Asia, and all the societal changes that have taken place as a result of both. As people look for comfort, they look for it in people and things. The sad part is they will not find comfort in anything this world has to offer. If a person wants comfort, they must go to God.

> *Blessed be God, even the Father of our Lord Jesus Christ, the Father of mercies, and the God of all comfort.*
>
> —2 Corinthians 1:3

That means money, sex, drugs, people, cars, homes, medication, counseling, and on and on do not possess comfort. That is why when someone experiences heartache and they search for that ease of pain through another avenue besides God, they will not find it.

I officiated my younger brother's funeral when he tragically died at the age of twenty-nine. The message God gave me concluded with how God is the only one that can bring comfort. Psalm 23:4 ends the verse by saying the same thing, which is that God comforts. Since He has all the comfort, you have to come to Him, and He will distribute it to you. The Shepherd has given you, the sheep, spiritual rest through salvation; you no longer want; you have physically rested; you have peace; your soul has been restored; you are on righteous paths; you glorify God; evil has not prevailed against you; you do not fear; He is always with you, and He defends and protects you. Now it is time to learn that God leads you to His comfort.

David makes a bold statement about God when He says, "they comfort me." While the rod and staff are used by the Shepherd because He loves you, they are also used by God to deliver to you His comfort. The Hebrew word used for "comfort me" is *nacham* (5162), which means comfort me, to be sorry, to pity, console, or avenge. Therefore, backing up a little in the verse, it could read: Thy rod and Thy staff they pity me, console me, and avenge me. True comfort from God takes into account pitying you, consoling you, and avenging you. His compassion and love for you cause Him to desire to comfort you. He knows your fragile frame.

> *Like as a father pitieth his children, so the LORD pitieth them that fear Him. For He knoweth our frame; He remembereth that we are dust.*
>
> —Psalm 103:13–14

The Lord is wanting to give you comfort but it is conditional. You have to meet the conditions God sets in order to receive His blessing. You must recognize that He is the source and come asking and seeking. You follow His leading while being willing and obedient to do what He commands you.

> *If ye be willing and obedient, ye shall eat the good of the land: But if ye refuse and rebel, ye shall be devoured with the sword: for the mouth of the LORD hath spoken it.*
>
> —Isaiah 1:19–20

Notice that if you are not willing and obedient, you will be devoured. God will not defend you with His rod and protect you with His staff because you are not allowing Him to shepherd you. Finally, it is important that you have "the fear of the LORD," which means to have a reverential respect for Him and His power. God says He will have pity on you if you fear Him. He will pity you and will bring comfort to you by His rod and staff. You are comforted because you know that nothing can take you out. There is strength in knowing that God will bring you through every good and evil situation. Furthermore, the Shepherd promises that even evil times will benefit you because you love Him, and He loves you.

> *And we know that all things work together for good to them that love God, to them who are the called according to His purpose.*
>
> —Romans 8:28

I have needed God's comfort many times in my life, and none was more apparent than my brother's tragic death. I received a phone call from my mother that woke me up abruptly out of my sleep. My mother, in a voice of shock, told me that he was dead. My mind started racing with questions as I could not understand and believe everything she was telling me. I knew the source of comfort was God, so I immediately started to cry out to Him for His help. I started to pray that God would give me the right words as to what to say because I knew my family and his friends would need a Word from God. I was willing to say whatever He told me. He spoke to me so clearly what I needed to preach at the funeral. I was to tell them that if they did not change their ways, my brother's death would be in vain. Furthermore, I was to tell them to run to God, be saved, and find their comfort in Him. It was a loving but strong message for everyone to wake up and stop playing with God. I knew it would be an emotionally tough funeral to get through with a fiery message. However, I obeyed God in everything. The Holy Spirit helped me deliver the message in such a loving but straight-to-the-point way as I have never experienced before. I had such a reverence for God that it caused me to check myself to make sure that everything was right between God and me.

The result I experienced was comfort. I could tell that God was lovingly wrapping His arms around me and supporting me during that difficult time. The Good Shepherd kept the enemy away with His rod. As the devil tried to make me fearful, worry, and have anxiety about everything the family was dealing with, God used His rod to destroy those attacks one by one. The Good Shepherd kept me on the right path with His staff. Anytime I was tempted to go down the what-if path or leaning to my own understanding path, He would gently use His staff to guide me to His Word that I needed at that moment in time. He has comforted me since with His love. I have learned that when I go through tough times, I can lean on

Him to comfort me. He will defend me from the enemy and protect me against myself, which is comforting.

Do you need the comfort that only the Shepherd can lead you to? If you have lived long enough, you will have your own difficult situation where you will need the comfort of God in a mighty way. I remind you to immediately go to Him. Go to your prayer closet and cry out to God. Tell Him how much you need Him. Remind Him that if He does not come through, everything will fall apart. The good news is He is willing to answer. He has the power. He knows exactly how to bring you through tragic situations and how to relieve you of all stress. You serve a gracious, loving, and comforting God. What a blessing of God!

Pray

"Dear Heavenly Father, help me to always run to You in the time of trouble for Your comfort. Please shelter me in Your loving arms and take all the pain and stress away. Let me rest in Your peace and comfort, knowing that You will defend me and protect me. May all this be done for Your glory alone. I ask all of this in Jesus' name. Amen."

Declaration of Faith

God, I thank You for comforting me.

DEVOTIONAL 13

Thou Preparest

Thou preparest *a table before me in the presence of mine enemies: Thou anointest my head with oil; my cup runneth over.*

—Psalm 23:5

My walk with God changed when I discovered that He has a perfect plan for me that includes prepared blessings. My life is not an accident. I have a purpose. I am not wandering aimlessly in this life trying to figure out what to do. The blessings of God in my life are not an accident; they are prepared. I have the Good Shepherd who is leading me along the paths He has planned in order to bless me. All I have to do is follow Him and let Him use me for His glory, and then I will experience all the great things He has prepared for me. I reap blessings in every area of my life on this earth and will in eternal life with Him. He has prepared all the same wonderful things for you because He is no respecter of persons.

For there is no respect of persons with God.

—Romans 2:11

The Shepherd has given you, the sheep, spiritual rest through salvation; you no longer want; you have physically rested; you have peace; your soul has been restored; you are on righteous paths; you glorify God; evil has not prevailed against you; you do not fear; He is always with you; He defends and protects you, and He comforts you. Now it is time to learn that God leads you to prepared blessings He has for you.

David says, "Thou preparest." The Hebrew word for "thou preparest" is *arak* (6186), which means thou preparest, arrange, or put in order. What is God arranging and putting in order for you? Verse five goes on to say, "a table before me," and I will discuss that in length in my next devotional message. What else does God prepare for you? The Word of God says that He prepares a lot of things: your creation, plans for your life, and the ordering of your steps. Your life is designed by Him to bring Him glory and bring you blessings. Before I talk about the prepared blessings, let me first generally explain God's arranging of your creation, life, and steps and how this psalm flows together so beautifully.

God planned for your creation. You are *not* an accident. He formed you while you were in the womb.

> *For Thou hast possessed my reins: Thou hast covered me in my mother's womb. I will praise Thee; for I am fearfully and wonderfully made: marvelous are Thy works; and that my soul knoweth right well. My substance was not hid from Thee, when I was made in secret, and curiously wrought in the lowest parts of the earth. Thine eyes did see my substance, yet being unperfect; and in Thy book all my members were written, which in continuance were fashioned, when as yet there was none of them. How precious also are*

Thy thoughts unto me, O God! How great is the sum of them!

—Psalm 139:13–17

God has planned a prosperous life for you.

For I know the thoughts that I think toward you, saith the LORD, thoughts of peace, and not of evil, to give you an expected end.

—Jeremiah 29:11

The Hebrew word for "thoughts" is *machashabah* (4284), which means thoughts, intentions, or plans. The Hebrew word for peace is *shalom* (7965), which means peace, prosperity, or health. God reveals through Jeremiah that He is planning ways to prosper His creation. This is an overarching plan of blessing. Also, the fact that God plans to prosper you is seen in the opening verse of Psalm 23 when it declares that "I shall not want." Furthermore, it is shown in many other verses because He leads the sheep to blessings.

God gets more specific as to having a plan to order your every step.

The steps of a good man are ordered by the LORD: and He deligheth in his way.

—Psalm 37:23

Also, the fact that God orders your steps is seen in the opening verse of Psalm 23 when it is declared that "The LORD is my Shepherd." Furthermore, it is shown in many other verses because He leads the sheep.

By now, you understand that the Shepherd is good. He plans to lead you to blessings. However, what the Holy Spirit,

Lord, has laid on my heart to show you through the words "Thou preparest" is that He is always looking to arrange a blessing in your life. In other words, He is always preparing a blessing. This is God's heart's desire: that His children be blessed. In true God fashion, though, He wants to put in order bigger blessings than you could ever dream of.

> *But as it is written, Eye hath not seen, nor ear heard, neither have entered into the heart of man, the things which God hath prepared for them that love him.*
> —1 Corinthians 2:9

Do you love God? Of course you do, so that means *big divine* blessings are prepared for you. The problem is people look at their flawed selves and think, "There is no way God will do this for me." Yes, He will. Not because of your righteousness, but because you are His child. You need to ask God for these prepared blessings and look for them all the time.

I no longer question if God wants to bless me because I know He wants to in great ways. I have been literally beyond blessed in every area of my life. Furthermore, I no longer make excuses for the blessings of God. Instead, I make sure to thank Him for His blessings and glorify Him with them. I am always looking around every corner every day for miracles, for favor, and for the divine blessings. I know what it is like to have the windows of Heaven to be opened and a blessing poured out so much that I cannot receive it all (Malachi 3:10). Is this why I serve God? Absolutely not. If God never did another thing for me, I would still serve Him. But this is His nature, a God who prepares blessings. Stop fighting it, and receive it.

Are you looking for what the Shepherd has prepared for you? Look by expecting; expect that every day and at any time,

God is going to do something big for you. That is faith, and it is a now thing (Hebrews 11:1). He is prepared to bless now, but He is waiting for His children that love Him to ask Him. You will not receive if you do not ask Him (James 4:2). Start asking and asking and asking. You are not being greedy. Ask God for His prepared blessings. What a blessing of God!

Pray

"Dear Heavenly Father, please give me immediately all the prepared blessings that You have for me. Help me to always be expecting and asking. May all this be done for Your glory alone. I ask all of this in Jesus' name. Amen."

Declaration of Faith

God, I thank You for leading me to Your prepared blessings.

DEVOTIONAL 14

A Table Before Me

Thou preparest **a table before me** *in the presence of mine enemies: Thou anointest my head with oil; my cup runneth over.*

—Psalm 23:5

One of my favorite things to do with my family is to go out to eat at different restaurants on Fridays with our Christian friends. There are usually sixteen people from four families that go, and trying to find a restaurant where we do not have to be separated can be difficult. However, most times, they are able to combine tables to accommodate us. We have great fellowship with interesting stories and a lot of laughter. There is always plenty of food, and everyone at the table is free from the cares of the world. It is simply a great time of fellowship and a blessing of God. Christians enjoying fellowship over good food brings glory to God.

The word food is mentioned over fifty times in the Bible. Food is eaten by humans and angels (Psalm 78:25). God, when He appeared before Abraham in Genesis 18:1–8, ate food. Obviously, God does not need food for His survival, but He eats. There was food in the ark of the covenant (Hebrews 9:4), and there is food in Heaven (Revelation 22:2). Revelation 7:16 indicates that in Heaven there will not be a need for food or drink to sustain life. However, there will be a marriage feast in Heaven that you will go to (Revelation 19:7–9). Why will there be a feast in Heaven if food is not necessary for life? This feast will be a time of fellowship and celebration with God. When you eat at this great feast, it gives glory to God. Even when you eat now on earth, it should be done for the glory of God.

> *Whether therefore ye eat, or drink, or whatsoever ye do, do all to the glory of God.*
> —1 Corinthians 10:31

The Shepherd has given you, the sheep, spiritual rest through salvation; you no longer want; you have physically rested; you have peace; your soul has been restored; you are on righteous paths; you glorify God; evil has not prevailed against you; you do not fear; He is always with you; He defends and protects you; He comforts you, and He has prepared blessings for you. Now it is time to learn that God leads you to enjoy His meals in safety.

God prepares a lot of blessings for you throughout your life. One of those blessings is seen here in verse five when it says, "a table before me." The Hebrew word for "a table" is *shulchan* (7979), which means a table or a meal implying a feast. The Hebrew word for "before me" is *panim* (6440), which means before me or face. Therefore, the text could read: a table with a feast on it in front of my face. The fact that the table is in front of one's enemies is significant, but I will talk about that part in the next devotional message. For now, I will focus on the question: why does God prepare a meal for you and put it on a table?

God created the human body on earth to need food and water, so eating and drinking are necessary. Think about how much time and energy you spend every deal meal preparing and eating. Unless you really enjoy cooking, making a meal can be a hard task. Here in verse five, God makes the meal for you. It is just one of the many blessings that God bestows upon His sheep. He does all the work, and there are no dishes left to wash. God prepares the food for you by blessing you with the means to obtain literal food. Food is something many take for granted. It is a blessing from God, and the righteous will always have bread.

> *I have been young, and now am old; yet have I not seen the righteous forsaken, nor His seed begging bread.*
> —Psalm 37:25

God is also speaking spiritually and figuratively in regards to the food that He prepares. Jesus says that you need food, but in order to live, you need His spiritual food, which is figuratively His Word.

> *But He answered and said, "It is written, 'Man shall not live by bread alone, but by every word that proceedeth out of the mouth of God.'"*
> —Matthew 4:4

Food can be prepared by God as a Word from Him in due season. For example, you may get a report from your doctor of a bad diagnosis. The enemy then starts attacking you with worry and fear. Then you might read your Bible, go to church, or watch a television minister, and the scripture about how Jesus bore the stripes for your healing (Isaiah 53:5) is read or mentioned. God prepared that spiritual food for you because that Word then brings forth life through a divine healing touch. You then can share a testimony of how God blessed you by healing you.

When the believer partakes in the act of communion, it is also a way that Jesus Christ uses Himself as prepared nourishment, which blesses you.

> *And as they were eating, Jesus took bread, and blessed it, and brake it, and gave it to the disciples, and said, "Take, eat; this is My body." And He took the cup, and gave thanks, and gave it to them, saying, "Drink ye all of it; For this is My blood of the new testament, which is shed for many for the remission of sins."*
> —Matthew 26:26–28

The food and drink you consume do not have to be on a table. You can carry it in your hands. I am sure you eat many meals on the go, just as I do. However, the Shepherd puts your feast on a table just like it will be when you get to Heaven. Why? That answer can be understood as to when you put your feast or meal on a table. You do not do this when you are driving or are busy. You do this when you are not rushed. As a sheep, you do this when you feel safe and secure. The Lord your Shepherd just led you through shadows of death where comfort was needed, and you are still in enemy territory. However, it does not matter. You can sit down, take your time, and eat a big meal because you dwell in safety. After all, the Shepherd will continue to watch over you, fight for you, and protect you while you eat.

I am blessed to have freezers full of food, which I enjoy in safety. However, greater than physical food is the spiritual food that God always gives me through His Word in due season, which I enjoy in safety.

> *A man hath joy by the answer of his mouth: and a word spoken in due season, how good it is!*
> —Proverbs 15:23

I can be going through a difficult situation or needing an answer to a problem, and God will send just the right Word for me. His spiritual food always solves every problem. I have also received His spiritual nourishment many times when taking part in administering and receiving communion. I always eat all that God has prepared for me in His safety. He is the provider that sets the table for feasting.

Do you need food from the Shepherd? He wants to bless you with a great feast. He wants you to receive nourishment physically and spiritually. He will do all the work. All you have to do is eat. Eat the physical food He provides and give Him thanks. Eat the spiritual food He provides and give Him thanks. Take part in communion as He directs you. Do all of this in the love and safety of your Good Shepherd. What a blessing of God!

Pray

"Dear Heavenly Father, please give me the meals You would have me consume. Help me to always give You thanks. May all this be done for Your glory alone. I ask all of this in Jesus' name. Amen."

Declaration of Faith

God, I thank You for allowing me to enjoy the feasts You have prepared for me in safety.

DEVOTIONAL 15

In the Presence of Mine Enemies

Thou preparest a table before me **in the presence of mine enemies***: Thou anointest my head with oil; my cup runneth over.*

—Psalm 23:5

I remember as a young minister not understanding how a Christian could call any person an enemy. I thought only the devil and demons could be enemies. As I grew in the faith, the Lord led me to understand that people will also be our enemies at times. The difference is in whom you wrestle.

For we wrestle not against flesh and blood, but against principalities, against powers, against the rulers of the darkness of this world, against spiritual wickedness in high places.

—Ephesians 6:12

The Greek word for "wrestle" is *pale* (3823), which means to wrestle, fight, or have conflict. Therefore, when you wrestle and fight, it is only to be against the devil and his demons, not flesh and blood.

Jesus says that you do not fight against the people who are your enemies.

> *Ye have heard that it hath been said, Thou shalt love thy neighbor, and hate thine enemy. But I say unto you, Love your enemies, bless them that curse you, do good to them that hate you, and pray for them which despitefully use you, and persecute you; That ye may be the children of your Father which is in Heaven: for He maketh His sun to rise on the evil and on the good, and sendeth rain on the just and the unjust.*
>
> —Matthew 5:43–45

The Greek word for "enemy" is *echthros* (2190), which means enemy, adversary, hated, or hostile. Jesus is saying people will hate you and will be hostile toward you. The devil will even use people to come against you in a variety of ways. However, you cannot hate the people, retaliate, wish them ill, or wrestle against them. Instead, you have to love them, bless them, and pray for them. In summary, I now know that while the enemies may be physical and/or spiritual in nature, I fight only the demonic. The Shepherd has given you, the sheep, spiritual rest through salvation; you no longer want; you have physically rested; you have peace; your soul has been restored; you are on righteous paths; you glorify God; evil has not prevailed against you; you do not fear; He is always with you; He defends and protects you; He comforts you; He has prepared blessings for you, and you enjoy His meals in safety. Now it is time to learn that God leads you to be blessed in front of your enemies.

The Psalmist teaches that the blessings of God will be enjoyed in front of those who hate you by saying, "in the presence of mine enemies." The Hebrew word for "in the presence of" is *neged* (5048), which means in the presence of, in front of, or before. The Hebrew word for "my enemies" is *tsarar* (6887), which means my enemies, to bind, tie up, narrow, or cramped. This implies that they are a captive audience. Therefore, this part of verse five could be read: in front of my enemies who are forced to watch me enjoy.

A question I asked God while writing this book is, why does He want your enemies to see you blessed? After all, God could have just blessed you in secret, and it could have just been a great moment that you and Him share. As I kept praying and meditating about my question, it became clear to me to go back to why we exist in the first place. Remember, we were created for God's glory (I covered this more in depth in Devotional Message Seven). If God allowed those who hate Christians or those who mistreat His children to win, would that glorify God? Furthermore, if God allows our enemies, which are influenced by evil, to win, then the devil wins. Does that glorify God? *No, no,* and *no!* God says that He will not share His glory with the devil, so anything that would bring glory to Satan is not of God.

> *I am the LORD: that is my name: and my glory will*
> *I not give to another, neither my praise to graven*
> *images.*
>
> —Isaiah 42:8

Since God will not give His glory to another, that means He will make sure that He gets it. One of those ways God receives glory is by blessing His children because you will in turn glorify Him. God knows that if His children are blessed, He will be glorified, and sometimes this is done in front of your enemies to even bring more glory to His name. Let me say that again: God receives glory when His children are blessed, and He even receives more glory when you are blessed in front of your enemies.

God abounds in love, patience, mercy, longsuffering, and goodness. This is why that person in your life who treats you like dirt over and over seems at times to get away with it. It can feel as if there is no end in sight. This is God giving time for that person to repent. This is where you are supposed to pray for these enemies of yours, do not wish them ill, but sincerely hope and pray they change. However, you notice that they are not changing, and you cannot take anymore. You cry out to God to move and please make them stop belittling you, making you feel worthless, taking advantage of you, and stealing your confidence. God hears your cry and says, "Since your enemies are not going to change, I will make them stop and will bless you in front of them." This is exactly what happened when the children of Israel cried unto the Lord when they were in bondage in Egypt.

> *Now therefore, behold, the cry of the children of Israel is come unto me: and I have also seen the oppression wherewith the Egyptians oppress them. Come now therefore, and I will send thee unto Pharaoh, that thou mayest bring forth my people the children out of Egypt.*
>
> —Exodus 3:9–10

God received glory in front of the Egyptians by striking them and delivering His children in a mighty way. He blessed His children in front of their enemy. Then He led them to the promised land. Notice though, before this happened, they cried unto the Lord.

Before you can receive this blessing from God of being blessed in front of your enemies, you have to humble yourself by crying out to God. It is an unfailing law of God that you cannot be exalted if you do not first humble yourself.

> *Humble yourselves therefore under the mighty hand of God, that He may exalt you in due time.*
> —1 Peter 5:6

Humility is saying, "I need God." It is the opposite of pride, which says, "I do not need God." Pride brings destruction.

> *Pride goeth before destruction, and an haughty spirit before a fall.*
> —Proverbs 16:18

Along with your humble cry to God, continue to set your love upon Him.

> *Because he hath set his love upon me, therefore will I deliver him: I will set him on high, because he hath known My name. He shall call upon me, and I will answer him: I will be with him in trouble; I will deliver him, and honour him.*
> —Psalm 91:14–15

Obeying God is one of the ways you set your love upon Him (John 15:10).

God has exalted my family and me many times in the presence of our enemies, and He has especially done this with my wife. My wife, Victoria, is gifted by God with people skills and business skills. She has a master of business administration (MBA) degree, completed business certifications through the Harvard School of Business, and worked many years for a big corporation. She started literally as a summer temp while in college and started to move up in her company. However, for a couple of years, she kept getting passed up for a lot of promotions. A high-ranking official told her that they knew she was great, but she did not do a good job bragging about herself and bragging about her accomplishments in the business. She and I both discussed and agreed that she would not go that way. Instead, she would be humble, continue to pray, and be a true example of servant leadership. Eventually, God moved in a new high-ranking official, and they noticed her God-given talents. The new official even said how they admired her humble leadership style. She was promoted numerous times and was over many of those that had been promoted wrongfully ahead of her. She had over 450 employees that reported to her and dealt with tens of millions of dollars. God was preparing her to run the growing ministry He blessed us with. She is now the chief operating officer (COO) of Ricky Branham Ministries and uses her God-given talents for the glory of the Lord.

Are you waiting for the Shepherd to exalt you in front of your enemies? Just like God promoted my wife, He will do the same for you. Love God with everything you have, humble yourself, and cry out to God. Pray for your enemies in the meantime and bind and rebuke evil and command it to leave in the name of Jesus. Remember, you are the head and not the tail (Deuteronomy 28:13). God will bless you so that your enemies are forced to witness it, which in turn will bring glory to God. What a blessing of God!

Pray

"Dear Heavenly Father, help me to love You and be humble by crying out to You. Please bless me in front of my enemies so that they may witness Your glory that I will give to You. May all this be done for Your glory alone. I ask all of this in Jesus' name. Amen."

Declaration of Faith

God, I thank You for blessing me in front of my enemies for Your glory.

DEVOTIONAL 16

Thou Anointest My Head with Oil

> *Thou preparest a table before me in the presence of mine enemies:* **Thou anointest my head with oil;** *my cup runneth over.*
>
> —Psalm 23:5

I heard God calling me into the ministry at the age of sixteen. When I graduated high school, I continued with my Christian education and became ordained at the age of twenty. At the same time, I went to college and became a registered nurse so I could financially support myself and a future family while continuing to minister. I mainly worked in the area of school nursing. What I did not expect was how much I would notice kids who felt unwelcomed, unloved, or unappreciated. I noticed it was some of the really nice good kids that some of their own family members, some teachers, or some students would prey on. They preyed on them by being hard on them or treating them unfairly. I believe sometimes, when this is done toward nice, good kids, it is rooted in jealousy and envy. The one who is mistreating them is jealous and envious because they see something in the other person that is nice and good when they themselves are not. Therefore, they manifest their unhappiness by being hard on them and treating them unfairly. Unfortunately, I saw some kids go through this. Obviously, to mistreat anyone, especially kids, is completely against God.

Jesus says not to offend kids or any child of His regardless of their age. Offending is causing them to stumble or stop serving Him. If you do, you need to repent, or there will be a severe punishment (Matthew 18:6). Jesus loves all people and especially kids. You need to love everyone and especially kids. Jesus welcomes all to come to Him (John 3:16) and especially wants kids to come to Him (Matthew 19:14). Jesus said to receive His children is to receive Him.

> *And whoso shall receive one such little child in My name receiveth Me.*
>
> —Matthew 18:5

My eldest son, Ricky, experienced this mistreatment with a few teachers and students. While he cannot walk on water—but who can?—he is an absolutely nice, good, and wonderful son who has always been a sincere follower of Jesus. He truly loves God and asks me questions all the time about the Bible. I could not originally figure out why some of his teachers and peers were so hard on him, jerkish in nature, and so unwelcoming toward him. Then when Ricky was eleven, God revealed to Victoria and me the reason when we were shopping with him. Ricky told me in the store that he knew he was going to be a preacher, but he was not sure what kind yet (pastor, evangelist, etc.). I told Victoria what Ricky had told me, and the light bulb went off in our heads. Besides people mistreating our son for no good reason because of their own issues, people sometimes mistreat him because he has a call from God on his life. They are being used as tools of the devil to try and discourage him. The devil is threatened by him because he is loved, anointed, and welcomed by God. Despite being mistreated, my son Ricky has graciously forgiven and prayed for the teachers and students who have done him wrong. Paul also recognized that evil was around him when he was doing good.

> *I find then a law, that, when I would do good, evil is present with me.*
> —Romans 7:21

The Shepherd has given you, the sheep, spiritual rest through salvation; you no longer want; you have physically rested; you have peace; your soul has been restored; you are on righteous paths; you glorify God; evil has not prevailed against you; you do not fear; He is always with you; He defends and protects you; He comforts you; He has prepared blessings for you; you enjoy His meals in safety, and you are blessed in front of your enemies. Now it is time to learn that God leads you to realize you are welcomed and approved by Him.

David teaches that you are welcomed and approved by God by saying, "Thou anointest my head with oil." The Hebrew word for "Thou anointest" is *dashen* (1878), which means to anoint or satisfy. The Hebrew word for "my head" is *rosh* (7218), which means literally the head. The Hebrew word for "with oil" is *shemen* (8081), which means oil, grease, liquid, or richness. Therefore, this part of verse five could be read: Thou satisfy my head with richness. This indicates that when someone's head is anointed, blessings are put on them. The blessings are plural because there are many including being welcomed and approved of God.

The anointing comes from God, Jesus, and the Holy Spirit. You can have an anointing in you (1 John 2:27) and upon you for the work of the Lord (Acts 1:8). The anointing is not something you can find, discover, or get on your own. This is verified through the meaning of the name Christ. In Matthew 1:1, the Greek word for "Christ" is *Christos* (5547), which means Christ, Anointed One, or the Messiah. The Hebrew word for "anointed" in 1 Samuel 2:10 is *mashiach* (4899), which means anointed or the Messiah. Both the Hebrew and Greek show that Jesus Christ is the Anointed and the Messiah. Notice that Jesus Christ is the Son of God who is the Anointed. It comes to you from above, so it has to be given to you. It is not in you by nature as it is in Christ. When the Psalmist says in verse five that "Thou anointest my head with oil," it is clear that the anointing has to come from the Shepherd that is leading. In other words, you have to be following Him in order to receive it.

The word anoint in the Bible has many deeper meanings, and sometimes it is used literally, figuratively, and spiritually. Sometimes it is a combination of some or all. The act of putting oil on a head is literal, but its meaning can be so much more than just the act itself. David probably used literal oil on his sheep to help keep insects and bugs off their faces. While the literal application of oil was used in many ways in the Bible and represented many things, it was used especially when putting into office the high priest. Aaron is a great example of this.

> *Then shalt thou take the anointing oil, and pour it upon his head, and anoint him.*
>
> —Exodus 29:7

The Hebrew word for "anoint" is *mashach* (4886), which means to anoint with oil, rub, or consecrate. The word "consecrate" here means and implies to be set apart by God. While this act upon Aaron was literal, it figuratively and spiritually meant he was the representative of God for a special purpose and was anointed with God's spirit. Therefore, the literal anointing of oil on the head can represent God's blessings of being welcomed and approved by God.

It was customary in Jesus' time, when welcoming and approving of someone to come into your home, to anoint their head with oil.

> *And he turned to the woman, and said unto Simon, "Seest thou this woman? I entered into thine house, thou gavest me no water for my feet: but she hath washed my feet with tears, and wiped them with the hairs of her head. Thou gavest me no kiss: but this woman since the time I came in hath not ceased to kiss my feet. My head with oil thou didst not anoint: but this woman hath anointed my feet with ointment."*
>
> —Luke 7:44–46

God's Word shows you in Psalm 23:5 that He wants to anoint your head with oil. God can anoint your head Himself, with a touch from the Holy Spirit, or He can send someone to anoint you with oil and lay hands on you as His representative. Once your head is anointed, God is saying that He gladly receives you and accepts you as good. In other words, you are welcomed and approved. There is such a freedom and peace in knowing that the world may hate you, but God loves you.

I have taught my son Ricky many godly principles from all the things he has experienced, and they may also apply to you. I have told him to let God continue to lead him in His righteous paths. There will be those who oppose him and do not want to like him. However, God has given him a higher welcoming and approval. Continue to pray and bless his enemies and keep his eyes focused on God. Know that God will handle those who continue to oppose him and who remain unrepentant because he is God's anointed.

> *He suffered no man to do them wrong: yea, He reproved kings for their sakes; Saying, Touch not mine anointed, and do my prophets no harm.*
>
> —Psalm 105:14–15

Are you ready to experience the welcoming and approval of the Shepherd? If you are completely welcomed and approved by the world, then I ask you to first check if you are being led by the Lord. You are not to be friends with the world because, otherwise, you will be an enemy of God (James 4:4). If this is the case, go back and re-read Devotional Message One and pray The Prayer of Salvation again. If you let the Lord lead you, you will find a true satisfaction that only comes when He anoints your head. Seek Him alone in your prayer closet and ask Him to anoint your head with oil and He will. The power of God can come alive in you and upon you with His anointed touch. The Shepherd says you are welcomed and approved. What a blessing of God!

Pray

> *"Dear Heavenly Father, help me to always remember that I am welcomed and approved by You. It is a gift from God, not anything that I have earned or deserve. May I always continue to be led by You and walk*

worthy of Your calling. May all this be done for Your glory alone. I ask all of this in Jesus' name. Amen."

Declaration of Faith

God, I thank You for welcoming and approving me.

DEVOTIONAL 17

My Cup Runneth Over

> *Thou preparest a table before me in the presence of mine enemies: Thou anointest my head with oil;* **my cup runneth over.**
>
> —Psalm 23:5

Victoria and I married in August 2007, and we were blessed to buy our first home shortly after in December of 2008. Our first child, Ricky, was born in April of 2009. It was a nice two-story home, and we had many great memories together as a young family in that home before we built our new home.

However, a bad memory from when we lived in our first home that still makes me squeamish is when our basement backed up with sewage water. Not to gross you out, but I could smell that something was not right. When I went down the basement stairs and turned the corner, sewage was everywhere. Victoria took Ricky and went to her parents' while I spent hours bleaching, mopping, and cleaning. To make matters worse, it happened again. The second time the sewage water was ankle-deep, and it completely ruined everything we owned in the basement. Sin does the same thing in a person's life. It stinks, permeates everything, and causes ruin. On the flip side, God's blessings can run over and permeate everything for good in a person's life. The Shepherd has given you, the sheep, spiritual rest through salvation; you no longer want; you have physically rested; you have peace; your soul has been restored; you are on righteous paths; you glorify God; evil has not prevailed against you; you do not fear; He is always with you; He defends and protects you; He comforts you; He has prepared blessings for you; you enjoy His meals in safety; you are blessed in front of your enemies, and you are welcomed and approved by God. Now it is time to learn that God leads you His overflow/riches.

First, know that everything belongs to God the Creator, and He can do what He wants with it.

> *The earth is the LORD's, and the fulness thereof; the world, and they that dwell therein.*
>
> —Psalm 24:1

God wants to give the earth to His children. After all, He does not need the stuff inside the earth.

> *The Heaven, even the Heavens, are the LORD's: but the earth hath He given to the children of men.*
>
> —Psalm 115:16

The nature of God is one blessing after another, and He enjoys giving to His children.

> *Let them shout for joy, and be glad, that favour my righteous cause: yea, let them say continually, Let the LORD be magnified, which hath pleasure in the prosperity of His servant.*
>
> —Psalm 35:27

David teaches that God is willing and wanting to give you His overflow/riches by saying, "my cup runneth over." The Hebrew word for "my cup" is *kowc* (3563), which means a cup or a lot. It is closely related to the Hebrew word *kis* (3599), which means a cup, bag, or purse. The Hebrew word for "runneth over" is *revayah* (7310), which means runneth over, overflow, satisfaction, or wealthy. To be wealthy means to be rich. Therefore, this part of verse five could be read: my purse overflows, or my bag is full of riches. Overflow is having enough to meet your needs and having some left over. God wants to give you overflow but is also willing and ready to give you His riches. Being rich is having an abundance of money. He will only give you His riches if He can trust you with His wealth.

Let me make a clear, bold statement: God really desires to make you rich. There is a "but," though. *But* God knows that not everyone can handle it. Let me now say it as one statement: God wants you to be rich, but He knows that not everyone can handle it. God will not give you His riches if you cannot handle it. In other words, if it causes you to falter in any way with Him or in any area of your life, He will not give it to you because you cannot handle it. Even if He does not allow you to become rich, He may bless you with overflow, which is enough to meet your needs and leave you with some leftovers, as long as you can handle that. God gives you what you can handle.

> *His lord said unto him, "Well done, good and faithful servant; thou hast been faithful over a few things, I will make thee ruler over many things: enter thou into the joy of thy lord."*
>
> —Matthew 25:23

Maybe you have been faithful and can handle God's overflow/riches, but you have not seen His blessings yet. Hold on, do not give up, keep being faithful, keep handling everything the way God would have you to, and keep trusting His plan. He is faithful and will come through in His perfect timing and will reward you when and how He sees fit.

If you are already rich and want to come follow Jesus, He will gladly receive you. He will want you to become right toward money in every way, if there is an area that is not right with Him (Matthew 19:16–22). Simply ask God to show you how to handle the money you have, and He will. Being rich is not a sin, but when you love money, that is where the sin is.

> *For the love of money is the root of all evil: which while some coveted after, they have erred from the faith, and pierced themselves through with many sorrows.*
>
> —1 Timothy 6:10

Do not lay up for yourselves treasure on earth but lay up for yourselves treasure in Heaven (Matthew 6:19–21). Meaning: give yourself fully to God and be concerned with eternal rewards. Maybe God has made you rich in order to use that money to help win souls for Him. God will continue to take care of you financially; just be obedient to His leading.

Why does God truly want you to be rich? First, remember that it is God's ultimate desire for you to be rich, but if it costs you your soul, then it is not worth it. Therefore, if God can trust you with wealth, He wants you to have it in order to win souls for Him. These are the last days before He calls His children home. Therefore, you need to win as many people for Jesus as you can. You are called to win souls and be witnesses for His kingdom, even if you are not a preacher (Matthew 28:19–20; Acts 1:8). The gospel is *free*. You can spread the message of Jesus for *free* in many ways: social media, word of mouth, praying, witnessing, sharing your testimony, letting your light shine, etc. However, it costs money to spread the Word through Bibles, keeping the church doors open, mission trips, humanitarian aid, printed material, television programs, radio programs, advertising, hospitality, and almost every other way of spreading information about Jesus Christ. God told me that He wants to bless me financially, make me rich, so it can be used to win a lot of souls for Jesus through the main avenue of my calling, which is television ministering. Television ministering can be expensive because of the cost of air time, production, closed captioning, and everything else that goes into making a program. The more networks you are on, the more money it costs. While it is not cheap, the rewards are eternal because of the souls that can be won for Jesus. Christian television is booming again, and God will continue to grow it as a way to win people for Him in these final days. My goal before I die is I want to see one million souls come to know Jesus through the ministry He has given me.

When God blesses you with His overflow/riches, you need to know and remember several things. First, always seek Him first.

> *But seek ye first the kingdom of God, and His righteousness; and all these things shall be added unto you.*
> —Matthew 6:33

Do not put emphasis on anything that distracts you from time with God, which includes friends, fame, money, or anything else. Instead, schedule time every day to be alone with

God in your prayer closet. I spoke about this in the "How to Read the Devotional Messages" section of this book. Second, be a giver. Give tithes, offerings, and sow financial seeds (Malachi 3:10–12; Luke 6:38; Galatians 6:7). Ask God to lead you so that you know how to give, where to give, and when to give. Then be obedient. Third, always remember God because He is your source.

> *But thou shalt remember the LORD thy God: for it is He that giveth thee power to get wealth, that He may establish His covenant which He sware unto thy fathers, as it is this day.*
> —Deuteronomy 8:18

I highly recommend you read all of Deuteronomy 8. Do not be like the rich man in Luke 12:16–21 who thought he no longer needed God since he was rich. Fourth, you cannot take anything with you when you die (1 Timothy 6:7), so do not concentrate on earthly things. Therefore, I repeat: do not lay up for yourselves treasure on earth but lay up for yourselves treasure in Heaven (Matthew 6:19–21). Meaning: give yourself fully to God and be concerned with eternal rewards. God will take care of you financially. Remember, when God blesses you with His overflow/riches: seek Him first, give as He leads you, He is your source, and you cannot take anything with you when you die.

I know I am called to be rich on earth, but I know my higher calling is to obtain eternal rewards. Eternal rewards are what truly matter to me. I do not want to buy more stuff because stuff does not matter. Furthermore, when I die, I cannot take any stuff with me, and why would I want to. I am going to Heaven. There are no "things" that I want to take from earth to Heaven. God wants to bless me financially for the main purpose of winning souls for Jesus. The Lord knows exactly how to make me rich so that it never gets in the way of my salvation or anything else.

> *The blessing of the LORD, it maketh rich, and He addeth no sorrow with it.*
>
> —Proverbs 10:22

I am working for God to win one million souls for Jesus Christ in my lifetime. Pray that God will continue to bless our ministry to make this happen.

Do you desire the Shepherd's overflow or the Shepherd's riches? Let God lead you. He wants to bless you so that you have more than enough. There are many great things that God can use you to do to build His kingdom, whether you have His overflow or riches. Remember, you can spread the message of Jesus for *free* in many ways: social media, word of mouth, praying, witnessing, sharing your testimony, letting your light shine, etc. The first goal for everyone should always be to make sure you make it to Heaven.

I just want to be clear: nothing is worth jeopardizing eternal life, so be careful with everything concerning money. The Bible does say that it is hard for the rich to make it to Heaven, so that is a great reason to be cautious.

> *Then said Jesus unto His disciples, "Verily I say unto you, That a rich man shall hardly enter into the kingdom of Heaven."*
>
> —Matthew 19:23

It can be hard for the rich to make it to Heaven because they may stop seeking God first, they may stop making God their source, they may stop giving, they may get focused on the stuff and things of the world, they may stop following the lead of the Shepherd, they may stop remembering God, or they may stop serving God altogether. If you are blessed with God's riches, it does not mean that you are not saved or that God cannot save you. Jesus can save anyone. He shows this three verses later when He says to His disciples that with God, all things are possible.

> *But Jesus beheld them, and said unto them, "With men this is impossible; but with God all things are possible."*
>
> —Matthew 19:26

Jesus is saying that He can save anyone, including the rich.

Do not make money a priority. Do not seek after it but rather seek God. Ask God to bless you with what He would desire for you to have. Ask Him to help you to be able to handle His blessings in every way. Let the Good Shepherd lead you. He will take care of you and will bless you with His overflow/riches that He wants you to have and that you can handle. He knows what is best for your life. What a blessing of God!

There are many Bible scriptures showing God's will to bless you with His overflow/riches. Here are some more for you to study: Genesis 1–2; Exodus 34:6; 1 Chronicles 4:10; 1 Chronicles 29:11–12; Nehemiah 1:11; Job 36:11; Psalm 84:11; Psalm 112:1–3; Proverbs 8:21; Proverbs 11:24; Proverbs 13:22; Proverbs 14:11; Proverbs 15:6; Proverbs 22:4; Proverbs 28:20; Ecclesiastes 5:19; Isaiah 1:19; Matthew 7:7; Mark 10:29–30; Mark 11:22–24; John 10:10; Galatians 3:29; 1 Timothy 6:17–19; 3 John 2.

Pray

"Dear Heavenly Father, please lead me into the blessings You have for me. Let nothing ever stop me from serving You and making it to Heaven. May all this be done for Your glory alone. I ask all of this in Jesus' name. Amen."

Declaration of Faith

God, I thank You for Your blessings of overflow/riches.

DEVOTIONAL 18

Surely

Surely *goodness and mercy shall follow me all the days of my life: and I will dwell in the house of the LORD for ever.*

—Psalm 23:6

One of my favorite words is *hallelujah*. That word just resonates with me when I hear it, say it, and sing it. The chorus of "Hallelujah" was popular at many Christian events back in the 1970s. I like to close many of my services by having the crowd stand and sing a chorus of "Hallelujah." The Spirit of God seems to flow in a mighty way when that beautiful word is sung to the Lord. The word *hallelujah* comes from two Hebrew words. The first word is *halal* (1984), which means to praise. The second word is *YHWH* (3068), which means the name Jah in reference to Jehovah the LORD. The King James Bible translates *hallelujah* as "Praise ye the LORD" (Psalm 111:1). It means to hail God the Creator and Redeemer. No wonder it is so powerful when sung as praise to God. In addition, Psalms 111–118 are known as the Hallelujah Psalms.

There are other words in the Bible that just speak to me in a powerful way: "suddenly," "immediately," "marvel," "now," "whosoever," and "whatsoever" to name a few. I am sure you have words that do the same thing to you. When I read Psalm

23, the word "surely" also speaks to me in that same powerful way. Surely God is faithful! The Shepherd has given you, the sheep, spiritual rest through salvation; you no longer want; you have physically rested; you have peace; your soul has been restored; you are on righteous paths; you glorify God; evil has not prevailed against you; you do not fear; He is always with you; He defends and protects you; He comforts you; He has prepared blessings for you; you enjoy His meals in safety; you are blessed in front of your enemies; you are welcomed and approved by God, and you are blessed with overflow/riches. Now it is time to learn that God leads you to realize He is faithful.

David teaches that God will do it by saying, "surely." The Hebrew word for this is *ak* (389), which means surely, certainly, or affirmation. Affirmation means that it is a fact. The Psalmist is definitively stating that the Shepherd will certainly do it. What will He do? He will make sure that goodness and mercy follow you as I will explain in the next section. The word "surely" also speaks to a very important part of God's nature: His faithfulness. He certainly will take care of His sheep. He, with assurance, will bless His sheep. He, as a matter of fact, will keep His promises because that is who He is.

> *Let us hold fast the profession of our faith without wavering; (for He is faithful that promised).*
> —Hebrews 10:23

God wants His sheep to know you can count on His Word and Him throughout all generations.

> *For ever, O LORD, thy word is settled in Heaven. Thy faithfulness is unto all generations: thou hast*

> *established the earth, and it abideth. They continue this day according to thine ordinances: for all are thy servants.*
>
> —Psalm 119:89–91

The fact that He is a faithful God to keep His Word is why you should believe in the power of prayer. You need to believe that if God says it, then so be it. Stop trying to overcomplicate things. Stop trying to figure out things on your own. God says it, so that settles it. You can see that God clearly loves you and is taking care of you, so why question His Word. If you question God's Word, you are questioning His faithfulness, which is part of the core of who He is. His sheep just need to know that He says "surely" about His Word.

I have seen the faithfulness of God to answer prayers in many areas, but especially in the area of sickness. I have prayed and claimed the promise that by the stripes of Jesus, you were healed (1 Peter 2:24). Notice that it is already done. God already said yes to the promise. My son Ricky was born with a hole in his lung (pneumothorax) and was literally turning blue and purple in front of me. It happened so quickly that the team of doctors could not do anything, and they said we would have to see if he would make it. I knew what to do. I cried out to God and prayed and claimed His promises. I watched as God literally breathed life into Him, and He became a miracle of God: the faithfulness of God.

My son Riley, around the age of five, had a grand mal seizure out of nowhere. It lasted over five minutes and was one of the scariest things I have ever witnessed in my life. He had two more within six months, and the doctor still could not figure it out, so they sent him for evaluations at a children's hospital. I told my wife that we were going to believe for a complete healing. That nothing is found. Soon as the doctor got his records and spoke with us, she prepared us by saying that she was certain he had epilepsy. Victoria and I agreed in prayer that we were not going to accept that. They ran all their tests, and to the doctor's surprise, nothing was found. She said she could not treat him because there was nothing wrong. He never had another seizure again, and He became a miracle of God: the faithfulness of God.

When we found out we were having another baby, we immediately started to pray and believe for a healthy baby in every way always. A man from our church told me that God told him that we would have a beautiful baby that would be like a yellow rose with no thorns. Sure enough, we had a beautiful, healthy little girl named Vera who had no thorns. We put her in yellow dresses a lot because of that prophecy, and she was a miracle of God: the faithfulness of God.

I could tell you countless more stories of how God healed my mother of brain tumors, how He healed me of headaches and a broken arm, how He has healed my family numerous other times, and of other healings inside and outside of our church. God showed me over and over His faithfulness to heal. When the coronavirus pandemic began in March of 2020, God taught me something about His faithfulness. He taught me to ask and believe that He is faithful to keep my family and me from getting sick. James 4:2 says that you have not because you ask not, so I asked God to make it so that my family and I no longer get sick. He faithfully answered. No coronavirus for any of us, and I am literally around thousands of people regularly. We all walk in divine health. When the devil tries to bring sickness, I bind and rebuke every evil spirit and command them to leave in Jesus name, and the sickness goes away immediately.

Is the enemy trying to get you to question your Shepherd's faithfulness? Do not lose hope. God has a perfect timing and a perfect purpose. God is faithful to answer in any area of your life. First, think about what you need or want. Then find a promise from God from His Word. Pray and believe that promise. Receive that promise by thanking Him ahead of time that it is done. Watch the faithfulness of God come to your rescue in due season. He certainly takes care of His sheep because He is a faithful Shepherd. What a blessing of God!

Pray

"Dear Heavenly Father, please help me to stand on Your promises, knowing that You are faithful to answer. Help me to believe You for the impossible. May all this be done for Your glory alone. I ask all of this in Jesus' name. Amen."

Declaration of Faith

God, I thank You for Your faithfulness and the faithfulness of Your Word.

DEVOTIONAL 19

Goodness and Mercy

Surely **goodness and mercy** *shall follow me all the days of my life: and I will dwell in the house of the* LORD *for ever.*

—Psalm 23:6

People need a lot of things in life. Maslow's hierarchy of needs says that physiological needs such as food, sleep, and water, are the most important and basic needs of all. Then safety, love, and a sense of belonging, self-esteem, and self-fulfillment are needs that every human has. You have to start with the basics before you can get to the higher levels. This logically makes sense in the fact that you first have to meet the most basic needs of a person before you can talk with them about meeting one's full potential. You can apply this to ministry in the sense that it is hard to win someone to Jesus if they are very hungry or do not feel safe. This is why many great Christian organizations and missionaries work first to meet those basic needs so that they will then be open to the message that they bring. In this devotional message, I will show you the reason God wants to give you goodness and mercy as a way to meet your wants and needs. The Shepherd has given you, the sheep, spiritual rest through salvation; you no longer want; you have physically rested; you have peace; your soul has been restored; you are on righteous paths; you glorify God; evil has not prevailed against you; you do not fear; He is always with you; He defends and protects you; He comforts you; He has prepared blessings for you; you enjoy His meals in safety; you are blessed in front of your enemies; you are welcomed and approved by God; you are blessed with overflow/riches, and God is faithful toward you. Now it is time to learn that God leads you to His goodness and mercy.

David says that God wants to give you two things: "goodness and mercy." The Hebrew word for "goodness" is towb (2896), which means goodness, pleasant, agreeable, beautiful, bountiful, ease, cheerful, best, favor, pleasure, prosperity, wealth, or precious. The word used in Hebrew is a word that is used very broadly. It covers so many things. The Hebrew word for "mercy" is checed (2617), which means mercy, goodness, kindness, piety, reproof, beauty, favor, good deed, loving-kindness, merciful kindness, or pity. Notice again the wide range of things that the Hebrew word for "mercy" covers.

God knows everything that you need. He knows everything that you want. He has a hierarchy, a plan, of what He wants to give you and how He wants to give it to you. The Psalmist knows that God is leading you to bring your needs and wants to be matched with what He wants to give you in order to accomplish His mission for your life. Therefore, nearing the end of this psalm, it was divinely inspired that, with certainty, He will give you goodness and mercy so much that it will follow you as I will show you in the next devotional message. Everything that God wills for you is in the two words: goodness and mercy. They are very broad words and all-encompassing. In other words, those two words incorporate every need and every want that you will ever have.

God is only a good God, and He never changes.

> *For the LORD is good; His mercy is everlasting; and His truth endureth to all generations.*
> —Psalm 100:5

> *Every good gift and every perfect gift is from above, and cometh down from the Father of lights, with whom is no variableness, neither shadow of turning.*
> —James 1:17

Imagine for a moment the goodness of God… What does God's goodness look like to you? It may look different to individuals, but I am sure to many of you, it includes something off this list: peace with God, a loving spouse, God-fearing kids, peace, joy, a nice home, a nice car, a job you enjoy, living a long life, and laughter. Now God says that is not big enough. You are not thinking and dreaming big enough. God says His Spirit is working in you, and it can do more than you think or ask.

> *Now unto Him that is able to do exceeding abundantly above all that we ask or think, according to the power that worketh in us.*
> —Ephesians 3:20

The great thing is the Hebrew word, towb, that God chose in Psalm 23:6 for "goodness" covers every good thing you could ask, think, and every good thing that God is willing to give.

The other thing you need in your life is God's mercy. One of the greatest examples of mercy in the Bible is the parable of a prodigal son (Luke 15:11–32). A brief summary: A father had two sons. The younger son says, "I want my inheritance," so the father gives it to him. The son squanders everything by living in sin. He does not even have food to eat. He decides to humble himself and go back to his father, hoping his father will have mercy on him. His father sees him from afar and runs to meet him and embraces him. The son repents and says how foolish he was. The father shows mercy and love to him by forgiving him, giving him a robe, a ring, shoes, and having a feast for him.

My summary does not do it justice. It is a beautiful story that needs to be read in its entirety. A parable is an earthly story with a Heavenly meaning. Our Heavenly Father never turns His back on you, but you can turn your back on Him. If you do go back to your life of sin, He is waiting and wanting to have mercy on you. Repent, confess, and accept Jesus Christ as your Lord and personal Savior. Pray The Prayer of Salvation found in Devotional Message One. He will embrace you and take you back into His family. The great thing is the Hebrew word, checed, that God chose in Psalm 23:6 for "mercy" covers every good thing you need for God to forgive you, save you, and love you.

I have experienced God's goodness and mercy firsthand. I can say with a certainty that God has been better to me than I have been to Him. I can summarize God's goodness to me by saying that He has always answered every prayer I have ever prayed in His way and in His timing. The ones that He did not answer exactly like I prayed, He ended up doing something greater than I had asked for. Furthermore, the joy and privilege I have received by being blessed to serve Him as a television minister, interdenominational evangelist, senior pastor, and an author is something that no amount of money could buy. The fact that God uses me for His glory is a result of God's goodness to me. The mercy of God has kept me on the right path since I have been fifteen. It has kept me on the right path because every time I have fallen short of God's glory and sinned, He has always been there to wipe the dust off of me and set me back on His paths. I am a committed Christian, a minister, and have a home waiting for me in Heaven solely because of God's mercy.

Are you experiencing the Shepherd's goodness and mercy? It covers everything you could ever want or need. Do not be afraid to ask God for His good things for your life. Ask Him to bless your family, your church, your co-workers, your neighbors, and your enemies. God wants to rain His abundant goodness in your life, and you have to be willing to receive it. Likewise, He wants to rain His abundant mercy in your life, and you have to be willing to receive it. Do not be afraid to go to God when you sin and ask for forgiveness.

> *If we confess our sins, He is faithful and just to forgive us our sins, and to cleanse us from all unrighteousness.*
> —1 John 1:9

He will have mercy on you. He promises. He is the Good Shepherd. What a blessing of God!

Pray

"Dear Heavenly Father, please help me to experience Your goodness and mercy. Help me to come boldly but humbly before You, always knowing that You want

what is best for me. May all this be done for Your glory alone. I ask all of this in Jesus' name. Amen."

Declaration of Faith

God, I thank You for Your goodness and mercy that abounds in my life.

DEVOTIONAL 20

Shall Follow Me

Surely goodness and mercy **shall follow me** *all the days of my life: and I will dwell in the house of the LORD for ever.*

—Psalm 23:6

I have always enjoyed most sports, but I especially enjoy basketball and cross-country. I still play basketball several times a week because I love the sport and so do my three kids. I do not run as much as I used to. In middle school, high school, and in my early twenties, I would have been called an avid runner. I ran a ton of 5Ks, a half marathon, a marathon, a Warrior Dash, and finished the Tough Mudder several times. My goal for most races was to win my age group, which I normally did or was close to. A couple of times, I got second place out of the entire race, and one time, I was blessed to win the entire race.

I was like most runners; when I arrived at a race, I would make sure I knew the course. I do not know why I put so much emphasis on this because I usually had plenty of people to follow, but it is the normal thing to do. In this part of verse six, David says that all those blessings that come from God's goodness and mercy will follow you. I picture this statement from a runner's perspective. In a race, you are following those in front of you, in the sense that they are ahead of you, and the runners behind you are following you, in the sense that they are behind you. In our spiritual walk, you follow the Shepherd because He knows the way, and God's blessings follow after you. I am excited to show you more about this in this devotional message. The Shepherd has given you, the sheep, spiritual rest through salvation; you no longer want; you have physically rested; you have peace; your soul has been restored; you are on righteous paths; you glorify God; evil has not prevailed against you; you do not fear; He is always with you; He defends and protects you; He comforts you; He has prepared blessings for you; you enjoy His meals in safety; you are blessed in front of your enemies; you are welcomed and approved by God; you are blessed with overflow/riches; God is faithful toward you, and you have His goodness and mercy. Now it is time to learn that God leads you, and His blessings follow you.

The Psalmist says with certainty goodness and mercy "shall follow me." The Hebrew word for "shall follow me" is *radaph* (7291), which means shall follow me, to pursue, hunt, or chase. Therefore, this part of verse six could be read: goodness and mercy chase me. This is the true meaning of the word "follow." Notice that this type of "follow" is not a behind-you-and-staying-behind-you-to-see-where-you-go. This is a hunt-you-down type of follow. God could have made it where you stumble on to His blessings, you guess and get lucky to find His blessings, or you have to work hard to get His blessings. Instead, God says, "I will make the blessings come after you, and they will catch you." The Lord, as your Shepherd, knows exactly the pace to lead you. He will go fast when He needs to and will go slow when necessary so that His blessings overtake you.

God gave the children of Israel the blessed promise that His blessings would overtake them if they would simply obey His voice.

> *And it shall come to pass, if thou shalt hearken diligently unto the voice of the LORD thy God, to observe and to do all His commandments which I command thee this day, that the LORD thy God will set thee on high above all nations of the earth. And all these blessings shall come on thee, and overtake thee, if thou shalt hearken unto the voice of the LORD thy God.*
> —Deuteronomy 28:1–2

Deuteronomy 28 goes on to tell of the blessings that will come upon His children for their obedience. These blessings can be summed up in God's goodness and mercy. Also, Deuteronomy 28 tells of curses that will come as a result of disobedience.

The Bible says you are the children of Israel (spiritually speaking) because you are the seed of Abraham through Jesus Christ.

> *And if ye be Christ's, then are ye Abraham's seed, and heirs according to the promise.*
> —Galatians 3:29

This means that the blessings promised to the children of Israel also belong to you because you are an heir. An heir is someone who is legally entitled to something. However, just because you are an heir, you still have to obey His voice in order to receive them. Other scriptures also show that what God did for the children of Israel, He will do for you: God is no respecter of persons (Romans 2:11), all scripture is given by

God for instruction (2 Timothy 3:16), and God never changes (Malachi 3:6). God has always promised that if His children obey, His blessings will overtake them. This is what Psalm 23:6 is indicating: you have been obeying because you are following the Shepherd. Now it is time for all of God's blessings, wrapped in goodness and mercy, to catch you.

God's blessings caught me. I have always sought God, but I started diligently seeking God's face and His ways like never before in March of 2020. God led me to do some Facebook ministry sermons during that time, which I did. On September 30, 2020, I met with a preacher who was on television. The preacher asked me if I had ever thought about television ministry. He did not know that when I was sixteen and I first started preaching, I wanted to be a television minister. When he asked me that question, something came alive in me and stirred again my desire to preach on television. I did not know how I could preach on television, considering I live in a small community and pastor a small church. I went to the Lord and prayed about it in my prayer closet. The Lord led me to the next step of contacting WGGN-TV 52, which I did. On October 21, 2020, exactly three weeks from when I was asked if I had ever thought about television ministry, I had a television contract with WGGN-TV 52 and was taping in their studio.

My television program, Ricky Branham Ministries, first aired on November 25, 2020, at 6 p.m. on WGGN-TV 52 in Ohio. The title of my sermon was "Remember Your Testimonies." My first radio program aired on WLRD 96.9 FM on November 29, 2020. On February 2, 2021 my program aired for the first time on WLLA-TV 64 in Michigan. On June 5, 2021, my program first aired nationally through GEB

Television Network. Since then, my television program has expanded to many more networks in the United States and continues to grow nationally and internationally. My program is in all fifty states as it goes out to a potential audience of over seventy-eight million people a week and growing.

God has amazed me with how He has wonderfully orchestrated everything in regards to television. He has given me a great Christian agent, the perfect church for production, an amazingly talented producer, a quality closed-captioning company to work with, and the list goes on. The television networks have been an absolute pleasure to work with in order to get God's Word out. All of this has been wonderfully orchestrated by God for this small-town preacher. God has done it in such a way that only He could receive the glory. God's blessings have literally chased me down!

Are the Shepherd's blessings following you? He wants His blessings to chase you down. Will you let Him lead you and set the pace so they will overtake you? How do you do that? By following His lead, asking, believing, obeying, and receiving. Take time to pray and seek His face, and His blessings will surely catch you.

> *But without faith it is impossible to please Him: for he that cometh to God must believe that He is, and that He is a rewarder of them that diligently seek Him.*
> —Hebrews 11:6

What a blessing of God!

Pray

"Dear Heavenly Father, please help me to obey You in all things so that Your blessings overtake me. I know this is part of Your plan, and I receive it. May all this be done for Your glory alone. I ask all of this in Jesus' name. Amen."

Declaration of Faith

God, I thank You for Your numerous blessings that have caught me.

DEVOTIONAL 21

All the Days of My Life

> *Surely goodness and mercy shall follow me* **all the days of my life***: and I will dwell in the house of the* LORD *for ever.*
>
> —Psalm 23:6

Living and growing up in Northern Ohio, I get to experience four seasons of weather every year. The joke in Ohio is that sometimes you might experience the four seasons in one day. Another joke Buckeyes make is, if you do not like the weather, wait just a little bit, and it will change. I enjoy the changes most seasons bring, but I thoroughly enjoy the continued warm sunshine and humidity of the summer. Summer never seems long enough because before you know, it is time for change again. Thankfully, unlike the Ohio weather, God never changes.

The fact that God never changes, unlike the seasons, is mentioned in the Bible.

> *Every good gift and every perfect gift is from above, and cometh down from the Father of lights, with whom is no variableness, neither shadow of turning.*
>
> —James 1:17

The Greek word for "variableness" is *parallage* (3883), which means variableness, change, or variation. The Greek word for "shadow" is *aposkiasma* (644), which means shadow or shading off. The Greek word for "turning" is *trope* (5157), which means turning, change, or mutation. All three of these Greek words are astronomy-related, which have references to the earth's seasons. James is saying that God does not change like the seasons. He is and always will be constant. Therefore, you will experience God's blessings of goodness and mercy every day. The Shepherd has given you, the sheep, spiritual rest through salvation; you no longer want; you have physically rested; you have peace; your soul has been restored; you are on righteous paths; you glorify God; evil has not prevailed against you; you do not fear; He is always with you; He defends and protects you; He comforts you; He has prepared blessings for you; you enjoy His meals in safety; you are blessed in front of your enemies; you are welcomed and approved by God; you are blessed with overflow/riches; God is faithful toward you; you have His goodness and mercy, and God's blessings follow you. Now it is time to learn that God leads you to experience His blessings every day.

The Psalmist says with certainty that the all-encompassing blessings of God, goodness and mercy, will chase you down "all the days of my life." The Hebrew word for "all" is *kol* (3605), which means all, any, the whole, or every. The Hebrew word for "the days" is *yom* (3117), which means day, daily, always, or continually. The Hebrew word for "of my life" is *chay* (2416), which means of my life, alive, or living. Therefore, this part of verse six could read: every day while I am alive on earth.

God desires, every day while you are living, to give you any blessing that you need or want. Why will He do it every day?

Because He does not change, He persistently desires to shower His children with the riches of His goodness and mercy. That means every day, you should be looking for His blessings by expecting to receive them. His goodness and mercy should be experienced every day. You do not wake up one morning and say to yourself, "Today, I am going to be hard on my kids. I am going to make their lives hard, miserable, and difficult simply because I can." Since you would never say or do such a thing, why would a God who is more loving say or do such a thing? You will do good to your children every day; how much greater will God do the same for His children.

> *If ye then, being evil, know how to give good gifts unto your children, how much more shall your Father which is in Heaven give good things to them that ask Him?*
>
> —Matthew 7:11

All of my devotional messages have shown that He is leading you down paths of blessings while you are alive. Psalm 23 is for the living, not for the dead. You have to be living to experience the "all the days of my life" blessings. If you are spiritually dead, you will not receive them. You can be spiritually dead from disobedience, unforgiveness, or any form of sin.

If you have gone astray (Isaiah 53:6), repent, confess, and accept Jesus Christ as your Lord and personal Savior. Do this by praying The Prayer of Salvation (Devotional Message One). Now pray Psalm 51:9–12.

> *Hide Thy face from my sins, and blot out all mine iniquities. Create in me a clean heart, O God; and renew a right spirit within me. Cast me not away*

> *from Thy presence; and take not Thy Holy Spirit from me. Restore unto me the joy of Thy salvation; and uphold me with Thy free spirit.*
>
> —Psalm 51:9–12

I expect every day for God to bless me in a great way. Not because I am worthy, not because I deserve it, and not because I earned it. I look for His blessings every day because I know that is what He is looking to do. Every day I look to bless my kids with a kind or encouraging word. Since I do this as an earthly father, God definitely does this to me as a Heavenly Father. I am not afraid to ask, and I am not afraid to believe. I go boldly to God with expectation.

> *Let us therefore come boldly unto the throne of grace, that we may obtain mercy, and find grace to help in time of need.*
>
> —Hebrews 4:16

Are you expecting and receiving the Shepherd's blessings every day? Now is the time to be on the lookout for His goodness and mercy. His goodness and mercy are found in every devotional message I have shared with you so far. Remind yourself that God wants you to have these blessings: spiritual rest through salvation, no longer wanting, physical rest, peace, soul restoration, righteous paths, glorifying God, evil not prevailing, no fear, never alone, defended and protected, comfort, prepared blessings, meals in safety, blessed in front of enemies, welcomed and approved, overflow/riches, faithfulness, goodness and mercy, being followed by blessings, and being blessed every day. What a blessing of God!

Pray

"Dear Heavenly Father, please help me to expect and receive Your blessings every day. I know this is Your will and plan, and I want to always be on the lookout for them. May all this be done for Your glory alone. I ask all of this in Jesus' name. Amen."

Declaration of Faith

God, I thank You for Your numerous blessings every day in my life.

BLESSING #3
Eternal Life

Dwelling in Heaven with God forever.

DEVOTIONAL 22

And I Will Dwell in the House of the LORD

Surely goodness and mercy shall follow me all the days of my life: **and I will dwell in the house of the LORD** *for ever.*

—Psalm 23:6

I find it sad that fewer and fewer Christians are assembling together especially knowing that Jesus could be calling us home anytime. God is clear that Christian believers should not forsake or leave behind the assembling together while on earth.

Not forsaking the assembling of ourselves together, as the manner of some is; but exhorting one another: and so much the more, as ye see the day approaching.

—Hebrews 10:25

The idea of going together to a place to serve God comes from Him. Different buildings are mentioned in the Bible as a place for His people to gather, fellowship, worship, and learn about Him: temples, tabernacles, synagogues, churches, and homes. Most Christians, including me, nowadays usually call this gathering together of Christian believers a "church." Church denominations are not a bad thing, but the denominational titles were started by man. However, the gathering together of believers was instituted by God.

The word "church" comes from the Greek word *ekklesia* (1577), which means church or a calling out. The idea is that it is a group that has responded to God's call. Therefore, everyone who has repented, confessed, and accepted Jesus Christ as their Lord and personal Savior is part of God's church. Jesus Christ is the head of the church (Ephesians 5:23). In Acts 7:38, the Israelites were referred to as "the church in the wilderness" because God had called them out. The church in Heaven is called "church of the firstborn" (Hebrews 12:23). Church, a gathering together of believers, can be held anywhere where there are at least two Christians gathered together (Matthew 18:20).

The important thing is to remember not to forsake gathering together with other Christian believers. You can get together at a church building or home or anywhere where you can serve God together. That does not mean you have to be in a church fifty-two weeks a year and three times a week. That does not mean you are in trouble if you miss church, get scheduled to work, or go on a vacation. Remember it says "not forsaking," which means to leave behind in the sense of doing away with. There are also shut-ins, many who do not drive, and others who simply cannot make it to gather together because they are so sick, which is why Christians should make house visits. God is loving and understanding. However, let me be clear, you should gather with your brothers and sisters in the Lord on a regular basis if you are physically able to. Many churches offer different days and times for services to help fit your work schedule and other family obligations. Make sure you make an effort to gather together as much as possible. Also, take your children because it is promised that they will continue to serve God when they are older if you train them in the ways of God when they are younger (Proverbs 22:6). My television and radio ministry is designed to be a supplement to feed those who truly cannot make it to gather together.

Gathering together at a church is not a chore; it is a blessing. This part of Psalm 23 promises life in Heaven. Assembling together and worshiping God in Heaven is one of the many wonderful things you will do when you dwell in Heaven. I want you to be ready for your dwelling in Heaven by knowing what life will be like. The Shepherd has given you, the sheep, spiritual rest through salvation; you no longer want; you have physically rested; you have peace; your soul has been restored; you are on righteous paths; you glorify God; evil has not prevailed against you; you do not fear; He is always with you; He defends and protects you; He comforts you; He has prepared blessings for you; you enjoy His meals in safety; you are blessed in front of your enemies; you are welcomed and approved by God; you are blessed with overflow/riches; God is faithful toward you; you have His goodness and mercy; God's blessings follow you, and you experience His blessings every day. Now it is time to learn that God leads you to obtain a future promise: dwelling in Heaven.

The shepherd says, "and I will dwell in the house of the LORD." The Hebrew word for "and I will dwell" is *yashab* (3427), which means and I will dwell, to sit down, to remain, or to settle. The Hebrew word for "in the house" is *bayith* (1004), which means in the house, family, or temple. David is saying that he will remain in the house of the Lord, which is living in Heaven. Notice that God's house is also called a temple. Therefore, it could read that he will sit down in the temple of the Lord. There will be church in Heaven.

The place where God dwells is in Heaven.

> *The LORD is in His holy temple, the LORD's throne is in Heaven: His eyes behold, His eyelids try, the children of men.*
>
> —Psalm 11:4

The New Testament also shows that God is on His throne in His temple in Heaven.

> *Therefore are they before the throne of God, and serve Him day and night in His temple: and He that sitteth on the throne shall dwell among them.*
>
> —Revelation 7:15

Jesus says that God has a place prepared for you so you may always dwell with the Father.

> *In My Father's house are many mansions: if it were not so, I would have told you. I go to prepare a place for you. And if I go and prepare a place for you, I will come again, and receive you unto myself; that where I am, there ye may be also.*
>
> —John 14:2–3

David loved to go to his place of worship to serve God. He wanted to do it all the days he was alive on earth.

> *One thing have I desired of the LORD, that I will seek after; that I may dwell in the house of the LORD*

all the days of my life, to behold the beauty of the LORD, and to enquire in His temple.

—Psalm 27:4

In Psalm 23:6, David is expressing that he is going to live with God in Heaven in the mansion prepared for him. He will be going to God's temple in Heaven because that is where the Lord is. He will be going there to worship Him, just like he did while he was on earth.

Life in Heaven will be greater than you could ever imagine, so you do not want to miss it. There are countless blessings in Heaven, and I am hesitant to say some because they are so numerous. Please read the book of Revelation sometime soon, and you will see. Here is a sample: you will know people in Heaven (1 Corinthians 13:12), you will have God's new name written on you showing eternal security (Revelation 3:12), you will have a mansion (John 14:2–3), there will be music (Revelation 5:8), there will be food (Revelation 19:9), you will reign with Him (Revelation 5:8–10), no more tears, death, sorrow, crying, or pain (Revelation 21:4) and there will be worship (Revelation 15:3–4).

If you receive all the blessings of Psalm 23 that are promised to you on earth, but you do not receive this promise to live forever in Heaven, you lost everything. Nothing can compare to the blessings of eternal life in Heaven. Jesus made this point.

For what is a man profited, if he shall gain the whole world, and lose his own soul? Or what shall a man give in exchange for his soul.

—Matthew 16:26

You do not want to gain the whole world and then be damned to Hell. Jesus gives a warning that you need to obey and that He better know you if you want to go to Heaven. In other words, He has to be your Shepherd and be leading you, or you will not make it.

> *"Not every one that saith unto me, 'Lord, Lord,' shall enter into the kingdom of Heaven; but he that doeth the will of My Father which is in Heaven. Many will say to me in that day, 'Lord, Lord, have we not prophesied in thy name? and in thy name have cast out devils? And in thy name done many wonderful works?' And then I will profess unto them, 'I never knew you: depart from me, ye that work iniquity.'"*
> —Matthew 7:21–23

There will be few that find eternal life because narrow is the way.

> *Because strait is the gate, and narrow is the way, which leadeth unto life, and few there be that find it.*
> —Matthew 7:14

I have to finish this life well, and that means making sure I have my priorities straight. I have to run this race of life to win the prize of Heaven (1 Corinthians 9:24). I want to dwell with God forever. I have been blessed with a great life, but none of this matters if I do not make it to Heaven. I know God has prepared a mansion for me, but I would take a shack or tent or whatever just to be inside those pearly gates. To dwell with the one who died for me and loved me while I was yet a sinner. To live a life of no more tears, death, or sorrow. I want to be there. I want to go to the Heavenly temple to worship God Almighty.

Do you have peace that you will obtain the Shepherd's ultimate blessing: to "dwell in the house of the LORD?" If not, then repent, confess, and accept Jesus Christ as your Lord and personal Savior. Pray The Prayer of Salvation (Devotional Message One), spend alone time with God, pray to God in the name of Jesus, worship Him, go to church, obey Him, and follow His leading. Commit yourself to Him, and He will keep you.

> *For the which cause I also suffer these things: nevertheless I am not ashamed: for I know whom I have believed, and am persuaded that He is able to keep that which I have committed unto Him against that day."*
>
> —2 Timothy 1:12

Finish this life well so that you can enter into eternal life hearing the words "Well done […]."

> *"His lord said unto him, 'Well done, good and faithful servant; thou hast been faithful over a few things, I will make thee ruler over many things: enter thou into the joy of thy lord.'"*
>
> —Matthew 25:21

You have the promise of living in Heaven and gathering together in God's temple with fellow Christian believers to worship Him who made it all possible. What a blessing of God!

Pray

"Dear Heavenly Father, please help me to make it to Heaven. I know that You are the way, the truth, and the life. I want all Your blessings on earth, but I want the blessings of dwelling in Heaven more than anything and anyone. May all this be done for Your glory alone. I ask all of this in Jesus' name. Amen."

Declaration of Faith

God, I thank You for leading me to my home in Heaven.

DEVOTIONAL 23

For Ever

> *Surely goodness and mercy shall follow me all the days of my life: and I will dwell in the house of the LORD* **for ever.**
>
> —Psalm 23:6

My grandmother, Lena Branham, who is now in Heaven, used to tell me when I was a kid how quick life goes. She said it seems to go quicker the older you get. How true I have now found that to be. When you are a kid, it seems like life is so slow. I remember being in high school, and it seemed like graduation would never come. Fast-forward, here I am, married with three kids, and life will not slow down. I always say I wish I could push the pause button. My kids are old enough to help take care of themselves but yet they still need Mom and Dad. I am not taking one moment for granted. I want to accomplish everything God has for me on this earth. Since life goes so fast, this may be why the Psalmist asks God to help him number his days.

> *So teach us to number our days, that we may apply our hearts unto wisdom.*
>
> —Psalm 90:12

If you are blessed to have seventy, eighty, or ninety years on earth, that is nothing compared to, as the King James Bible says it, "for ever." The Shepherd has given you, the sheep, spiritual rest through salvation; you no longer want; you have physically rested; you have peace; your soul has been restored; you are on righteous paths; you glorify God; evil has not prevailed against you; you do not fear; He is always with you; He defends and protects you; He comforts you; He has prepared blessings for you; you enjoy His meals in safety; you are blessed in front of your enemies; you are welcomed and approved by God; you are blessed with overflow/riches; God is faithful toward you; you have His goodness and mercy; God's blessings follow you, and you experience His blessings every day. He has given you a future promise of dwelling in Heaven. Now it is time to learn that God leads you to obtain another future promise: "for ever."

The Psalmist says, "and I will dwell in the house of the LORD for ever." The Hebrew word for "for ever" is *orek* (753), which means forever, length, or long. "For ever" means exactly what you think; it is forever. It is time without end. Other words in the Bible like "eternal," "eternity," or "everlasting" convey the same idea and meaning as "for ever." The Shepherd led David and has led you to all His blessings on earth throughout this psalm. He then ends purposely with this verse about being in Heaven forever. God is culminating David's journey and your journey by giving the biggest blessing yet that you will live in Heaven with God forever. You never have to leave God and His blessings.

Eternal life is dwelling in Heaven with God forever.

> *And this is life eternal, that they might know thee the only true God, and Jesus Christ whom thou hast sent.*
> —John 17:3

It is the plan of God for everyone to have everlasting life.

> *For God so loved the world, that He gave His only begotten Son, that whosoever believeth in Him should not perish, but have everlasting life.*
> —John 3:16

There is an eternal punishment for those who do *not* repent, confess, and accept Jesus Christ as their Lord and personal Savior. Eternal punishment is living in Hell, separated from God forever.

> *Jesus saith unto him, "I am the way, the truth, and the life: no man cometh unto the Father, but by me."*
> —John 14:6

> *And these shall go away into everlasting punishment: but the righteous into life eternal.*
> —Matthew 25:46

The good news is you and I are going to Heaven. We have met the conditions of salvation. We are going to stay in Heaven forever and worship Him while enjoying His blessings. Here is a simple illustration I use to help explain the length of eternal life: Take the largest mountain in the world, Mt. Everest, and turn it into sand. Take the largest ocean in the world, the Pacific Ocean, and remove all the water. Then take all that sand and put it where the ocean was. Then have a bird come every million years to take away one grain of sand until all the sand is gone. That is just the beginning of eternal life.

Are you ready for the Shepherd to take you to Heaven forever? I am, but I do have family and friends that I still want to be saved first. I am sure you do too. I am so excited though because you and I have chosen to let the Good Shepherd lead us. Now anytime you ever hear about Psalm 23, you will know it is for the living. It is filled with God's blessings: salvation, overflow, and eternal life. I know this book contained a lot of material. You may need to reread it or break it down into smaller sections, and I encourage you to do so. Please share it with all of your family, friends, and church family. God, out of His vast abundance, is big enough to bless you and the eight billion people in the world. God owns it all, and He wants to share it with you and everyone. God is willing and waiting for people to receive it.

Let's look one more time at the blessings the Shepherd has given and will give you, the sheep, that come from Psalm 23: spiritual rest through salvation, no longer wanting, physical rest, peace, soul restoration, righteous paths, glorifying God, evil not prevailing, no fear, never alone, defended and protected, comfort, prepared blessings, meals in safety, blessed in front of enemies, welcomed and approved, overflow/riches, faithfulness, goodness and mercy, being followed by blessings, being blessed every day, living in Heaven, and eternal life. What a blessing of God!

I love you, and God bless you. Please pray for my family and me, and we will do the same for you.

Pray

"Dear Heavenly Father, I want to accomplish all that You have for me on earth. I trust You. I will follow You all the days of my life. Please lead me into eternal life when it is appointed for me to go. May all this be done for Your glory alone. I ask all of this in Jesus' name. Amen."

Declaration of Faith

God, I thank You for giving me eternal life.

HOW THE LORD BECAME MY SHEPHERD

From the Beginning

*"For I know the thoughts that I think toward you,"
saith the LORD, "thoughts of peace, and not of evil, to
give you an expected end."*

—Jeremiah 29:11

My mother, Ellen, noticed that I had a calling in my life before I was born. She remembers that I constantly moved in her belly during church services as though I were praising the Lord. When I was around the age of two, my parents and I had a direct encounter with an angel from God and Satan. My mother abruptly awoke out of her sleep and saw me standing at the entrance of her bedroom. I was rubbing my eyes, and she told me to come and get in bed. However, she unexpectedly noticed an angelic being, clearly not from this world, standing behind me, waving his hands. The being was a male angel, and there was a bright light shining around him. He was translucent, wearing a long white robe with wide sleeves. Suddenly my mother noticed that it was not me standing there but that it was my spirit. She woke up my father, but he did not see anything.

My mother started praying that I would come and get in bed with them if I was going to live. She prayed hard until she somehow fell back asleep. Without warning, she was awakened to me crawling in bed with them. The angel appeared to her in the same spot again. She woke my father again, but he still did not see the angel. Then I said, "Mommy, I see, I see, a man in white," which surprised my parents because that was before I could speak full sentences and before I knew my colors. My parents were amazed, and, somehow, everyone fell asleep.

My father then dreamed that an angel touched the bed, and it began to spin. My father woke everyone up, and this time, my mother saw a man dressed in all black, with red eyes, and his skin looked like charcoal. He stared at all three of us and then walked out of the trailer through the wall. My father did not see him, but he believed what my mother saw. My mother believed that this series of events meant that God had something special planned for me, but the devil was mad and wanted to stop it. It was shortly after that incident that my parents went through a divorce, no doubt an attack of the devil.

Both of my parents would later remarry other people when I was about eight. I went to church with my mother and stepfather, and father and stepmother when they went. I can recall most of those times. I can remember seeing the people, hearing the music, and listening to the preachers. I can even remember some of the candle smells and giggling at some of the strange and vibrant colored suits that some of the men wore that were popular at the time. The main thing I recall was how nice everyone was to me.

God Uses My Grandparents

As I got older, I started to spend more time with my paternal grandparents, Robert and Lena Branham. They were both originally from Eastern Kentucky, and they both moved to

Northern Ohio when they were young. They were both raised in the ways of God. They met and married at a young age. They loved God, Jesus, and the Holy Spirit. They loved going to church. I started going with them every opportunity I could because they exuded the love of God, and it drew me to them.

I went to church with my grandparents two to three times a week. They would get there early to open the church doors, turn on the lights, and to make sure everything was just perfect and ready to go. My wonderful Sunday school teachers taught me the Ten Commandments, the Twelve Beatitudes, how Jesus loved me, and how enjoyable it is to serve God. I participated in church plays, which was definitely not my strong suit. At some of the services, I would take a nap in my pew. Church provided for some of the best napping because it was the most peaceful place a kid could be. However, most of the time, I was a giant sponge soaking in everything I could about God. I began to understand what it meant to have a relationship with God.

My grandparents were a wonderful example of a happily married couple who put God first in every way. They were hard workers, kind, and selfless.

> *Let your light so shine before men, that they may see your good works, and glorify your Father which is in Heaven.*
>
> —Matthew 5:16

They let their light shine just like Christ taught in the Gospels. I saw their good works, and so did others. They did not boast about their good works but rather just did them in a loving way. I watched them and wanted to be like them when I grew up: a strong in the faith family who loved the Lord.

God Speaks to Me Directly

In 1998 when I was fifteen, I began to slowly drift away from God. One night, when I was on the way back home after hanging out with friends, I was in a bad car accident. I asked the EMT if I was going to live as I was being rushed to the hospital. The EMT plainly said, "I don't know." I was bleeding profusely from a head trauma. The hospital did a CT scan of my head, and I was put in a dark, quiet room while they called my family in.

As I lay in that room, I noticed that God was speaking to me. It was not an audible voice but a still small voice that was pressing upon my heart and mind. It was hard to explain, but I knew it was God.

> *"Behold, I stand at the door, and knock: if any man hear my voice, and open the door, I will come in to him, and will sup with him, and he with Me."*
>
> —Revelation 3:20

God was knocking on the door of my heart, and He wanted me to let Him in all the way. God started speaking to me, telling me that if I had died, I would have gone to Hell because I had turned my back on Him. That may sound like God was being harsh, but He was not. God told me in such a loving way that it caused me to want to change and be fully committed to Him like never before. I told God if He would spare me that, I would serve Him all the days of my life. In the stillness of the room, all alone, I repented, confessed, and accepted Jesus Christ as my Lord and personal Savior.

The doctor came back into the room to further examine me. The doctor said I could have died instantly based on the way my face struck the car upon impact. He said I would need to see a plastic surgeon for reconstructive surgery on my nose and face. The doctor called me a miracle. I knew it was an act of God that I was alive. God spared me, saved me, and finished His healing work in me. I healed in such a great way that I never had to have any kind of reconstructive surgery.

Called to Preach

After my car accident, I started going to church again like never before. I went with my grandparents, with friends, by myself, and with anyone else who would go. I tried my best to be there whenever the doors were open. On April 7, 1999, at the age of sixteen, during a Wednesday night youth church service, I felt God speak to me directly again. God impressed upon my heart that I was called to preach. I knew it was God speaking to me again.

I hurried home that night to tell my mother the good news. She gave me the advice not to tell anyone but to wait and see if God really was calling me to minister. Shortly after that, evangelist and Senior Pastor Rev. Ralph Farmer asked me when I was going to preach for him at his church. That same day, a musician named R. B. Fallen asked me when I was going to preach. I asked R. B. how he knew that I was called to preach. R. B. smiled and said, "I can just tell." I knew that God used Rev. Ralph Farmer and R. B. Fallen to confirm my calling.

On May 14, 1999, at Rev. Ralph Farmer's church in North Fairfield, Ohio, I preached my first sermon to a packed country church with 105 people in attendance. The sermon was titled "Trust." It lasted twelve minutes. One person repented, confessed, and accepted Jesus Christ as their Lord and personal

Savior. It was evident to everyone in attendance that I was truly called by God to preach. From that point on, ministers from all denominations began to contact me about preaching at their church. Rev. Ken Gifford, a local Methodist minister, took me under his wings and helped me in a variety of areas regarding ministry. I continued to minister, grow in the faith, and began my Christian studies. I was ordained in 2003, at the age of twenty, by Ripley Chapel, a non-denominational church. I became an interdenominational evangelist, filling in for all denominations, spreading the good news of Jesus Christ.

God Blesses Me with a Wife

In 2004 at the age of twenty-one, I graduated from North Central State College (NCSC) as a registered nurse (RN) in order to help supplement my income. In the fall, I started praying that God would send me the wife that He had prepared for me. I read Christian books about love and prayed a lot on this topic. God was putting this desire in me for a reason. I had peace that God would send me a wife in His perfect timing.

Later in 2004, I started seeing this beautiful woman around town. She had a contagious smile, dark brown hair, and dark brown eyes. I saw her at the hospital while I took care of her father, I saw her at the tire shop of all places, and other places around our local community. I knew exactly who she was. Her name was Victoria, and she had been a senior in high school when I was a freshman. I thought in high school how beautiful she was. However, I was a freshman, so I did not even try talking with her. Also, I had worked with her in 2002 at Pepperidge Farm on one of the packaging lines while we were on summer break from college. The funny thing is I worked right beside her, and we did not even talk. She was not a Christian when we worked together, so it was not God's timing yet for us to get to know each other. God was preparing her first to become a Christian, and she did. By the time I started seeing her around town a lot, she had become a committed follower of Jesus Christ. I would later find out that she became a Christian when she heard television minister Dr. Creflo Dollar give an altar call. She got on her knees in her apartment and right there on the spot repented, confessed, and accepted Jesus Christ as her Lord and personal Savior. It changed her life. She started going to church and growing greatly in the faith.

I made up my mind that the next time I saw her that I was going to ask her out. As God would have it, on December 20, 2004, I would get my chance. I went to Cleveland, Ohio, with my friend Ryan, and I was supposed to be back in town for a family event by 6:00 p.m. However, the roads were not good, and there was no way I was going to be back in time. As I got closer to home, Ryan asked if we could stop at a Barnes & Noble so that he could get a book. I agreed because I knew I was not going to be able to make it to my family event on time.

Almost as soon as I walked through the doors at Barnes & Noble, there Victoria was. God quickly reminded me how I promised myself that I was going to ask her out the next time I saw her. God was not going to let me forget or chicken out. I mustered up the confidence and asked her if she would like to go out sometime. I thought in my head there was no chance, but I had to at least ask so I would know. She smiled and said she would. I could not believe it. We stayed and talked for over an hour at the store until she had to leave to get ready for work because she now worked third shift full-time at Pepperidge Farm. Ryan and I left Barnes & Noble and stopped at another store before heading closer to home to get gas. There Victoria was at the gas station. Victoria and I laughed, smiled, and waved. Four days later, on December 24, 2004, Victoria and I had our first official date at a Christmas Eve church service. We married on August 11, 2007, with Rev. Ken Gifford performing the ceremony.

Pastoring

Victoria and I went all over evangelizing. One particular church that I preached at regularly and I was licensed through, Ripley Chapel, asked me if I would fill in for them long-term until they found a pastor. In January of 2008, I started to fill in for them with the understanding that they would not call me pastor. I did not want to be called a pastor because I viewed myself only as an evangelist. However, as the head of the church board introduced me to the congregation, he called me the pastor. I continue to be their senior pastor to this day while continuing to evangelize interdenominationally.

Family and Education

In 2009 Victoria and I were blessed with our first son, Ricky. In 2011 we were blessed with another son, Riley. In 2013 we were blessed with a daughter, Vera. God had expanded our family and provided the perfect setting for us to raise our children in the Lord. God started teaching us what a godly home looked like. After we were married and while our kids were young, I continued my education with the School of Ministry and the Church of God receiving the Church of God's licensure and ordination as a minister. I also completed my bachelor of arts

(BA) degree in organizational management and my master of business administration (MBA) degree from Malone University. Victoria completed her master of business administration (MBA) degree from Malone University. She also completed business certifications through the Harvard School of Business.

Television and Radio

I have always had a desire to be a television minister, ever since God called me to preach. The fourth message I ever preached, which was on July 6, 1999, was on television because I was an invited guest by Rev. Ralph Farmer. It was on WGGN-TV 52 in Northern Ohio. That would be the only time I would preach on television until over twenty years later. I had stopped seeking God about becoming a television minister. However, God, in His infinite wisdom, mercy, and grace, did not forget about the dream that He had placed in my heart long ago.

On September 30, 2020, I met with a preacher who was on television. The preacher asked me if I had ever thought about television ministry. He did not know that when I was sixteen and I first started preaching, I wanted to be a television minister. When he asked me that question, something came alive in me and stirred again my desire to preach on television. I did not know how I could preach on television, considering I live in a small community and pastor a small church. I went to the Lord and prayed about it in my prayer closet. The Lord led me to the next step of contacting WGGN-TV 52, which I did. On October 21, 2020, exactly three weeks from when I was asked if I had ever thought about television ministry, I had a television contract with WGGN-TV 52 and was taping in their studio.

My television program, Ricky Branham Ministries, first aired on November 25, 2020, at 6 p.m. on WGGN-TV 52 in Ohio. The title of my sermon was "Remember Your Testimonies." My first radio program aired on WLRD 96.9 FM on November 29, 2020. On February 2, 2021, my program aired for the first time on WLLA-TV 64 in Michigan. On June 5, 2021, my program first aired nationally through GEB Television Network. Since then, my television program has expanded to many more networks in the United States and continues to grow nationally and internationally. My program is in all fifty states as it goes out to a potential audience of over seventy-eight million people a week and growing.

God has amazed me with how He has wonderfully orchestrated everything in regards to television. He has given me a great Christian agent, the perfect church for production, an amazingly talented producer, a quality closed-captioning company to work with, and the list goes on. The television networks have been an absolute pleasure to work with in order to get God's Word out. All of this has been wonderfully orchestrated by God for this small-town preacher. God has done it in such a way that only He could receive the glory. God's blessings have literally chased me down!

Master of Theology (ThM) and Doctor of Ministry (DMin)

I thought I was done with college at least from the standpoint of pursuing degrees. I had originally wanted to obtain my doctorate but thought maybe it was not meant to be, so I gave up on the idea. However, God clearly showed me that He wanted me to go to college for my doctorate and opened the door for me to do so. I graduated from the Christian Bible Institute and Seminary (CBIS) with a master of theology (ThM) degree and a doctor of ministry (DMin) degree in April of 2022. I noticed a theme with God: God does the impossible. He is a doctor that specializes in the impossible. I had a dream to become a television minister when I was first called to preach, but I had given up on that. It seemed impossible. I had a desire to obtain my doctorate, but I had given up on that. It seemed impossible. However, God made both things happen in His time. God does the impossible. He is a doctor that specializes in the impossible.

Going Forward

I continue to minister all over, spreading the good news of Jesus Christ as a television minister, interdenominational evangelist, senior pastor, and author. Ricky Branham Ministries (RBM) desires to reach the lost, edify the saints, and minister to people of all ages and in all walks of life for the glory of Jesus Christ. God can do the impossible, and God desires to do the impossible. Matthew 19:26 says, "But Jesus beheld them, and said unto them, With men this is impossible; but with God all things are possible."

My television program, Ricky Branham Ministries, is on many networks in the United States and continues to grow nationally and internationally. My program is in all fifty states as it goes out to a potential audience of over seventy-eight million people a week and growing. I am an interdenominational evangelist who travels all over and preaches at all denominations and churches that proclaim Jesus Christ as Lord and personal Savior. I am the senior pastor of a non-denominational church, Ripley Chapel. I continue to serve and preach at my home church when I am not traveling. I will leave listeners with a message from God that is timely, memorable, and applicable. If you would like to have me speak at your church or ministry event, please contact Ricky Branham Ministries through my website: www.rickybranham.com.

BIBLIOGRAPHY

Bible Hub online. https://biblehub.com/.

Strong, James. *The new Strong's exhaustive concordance of the Bible: with main concordance, appendix to the main concordance, topical index to the Bible, dictionary of the Hebrew Bible, dictionary of the Greek Testament.* Nashville: T. Nelson Publishers, 1996.

COMING SOON

Be on the lookout for more books in the "Readings for Your Prayer Closet" Devotional Message Series and other books by Dr. Ricky Branham.

CONTACTS/TELEVISION/ SOCIAL MEDIA

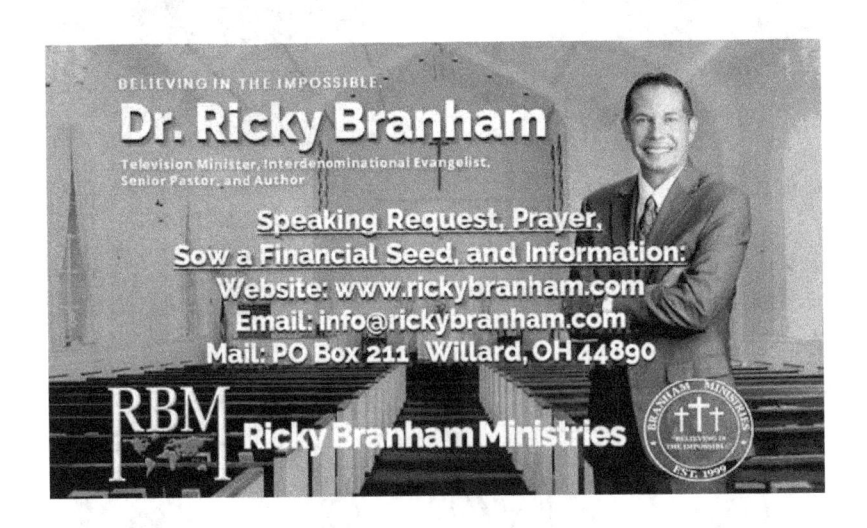

BELIEVING IN THE IMPOSSIBLE.
Dr. Ricky Branham
Television Minister, Interdenominational Evangelist, Senior Pastor, and Author

Speaking Request, Prayer, Sow a Financial Seed, and Information:
Website: www.rickybranham.com
Email: info@rickybranham.com
Mail: PO Box 211 Willard, OH 44890

RBM Ricky Branham Ministries

Television (All 50 States & Expanding):

- Search on your television for your local TV listing: Ricky Branham Ministries

RBM Ricky Branham Ministries

RBM
Ricky Branham Ministries

BRANHAM MINISTRIES
"BELIEVING IN THE IMPOSSIBLE"
EST. 1999

CPSIA information can be obtained
at www.ICGtesting.com
Printed in the USA
BVHW060327121022
649129BV00002B/4